D1313192

The Sea Angler's Guide to
TOP MARKS

emap active

Acknowledgements
Editor: Mel Russ
Compilation: Cliff Brown
Photographs: Sea Angler library
Maps: Steve Diggle and Ricci Cox

ISBN 0-9533087-9-0

Produced by
Publishing Promotions
1 High Street
Princes Risborough
Buckinghamshire
HP27 0AG

Published by
EMAP Active Ltd
Bushfield House
Orton Centre
Peterborough
PE2 5UW

The Sea Angler's Guide to
TOP MARKS

Welcome
to the nation's Top Marks

Sea anglers are always hungry for information and one
of their top priorities is finding new places to fish.
That's where our *Top Marks* book can help because it
points you in the direction of dozens of fishing spots
that all have proven track records.

This unique *Sea Angler* book contains almost 180 marks,
which begin in Northumberland, travel south down
the North Sea coast, through the English Channel to
Cornwall, turns east up the Bristol Channel, then
west along the South Wales coast.

Our journey of discovery then heads north along the
Welsh coast and continues on to Cumbria, briefly
touching the Isle of Man. Crossing the Scottish border,
our *Top Marks* guide touches all the popular fishing
grounds on the west, north and east coasts.

Essential information includes an overview of each mark,
including the best tides to fish, the species you can
catch, best baits, tackle that works on the marks, details
on how to reach it by road, including a local area map,
and a tackle shop contact for more information and bait.

Our research constantly throws up the fact that
you all want more information on where to fish, and
the team at *Sea Angler* hope we have fulfilled that
need by publishing this *Top Marks* guide for
the nation's sea anglers.

Mel Russ
Editor, *Sea Angler* magazine

Contents

Northumberland	10
Tyne & Wear	16
County Durham	22
Cleveland	28
Yorkshire	34
Lincolnshire	42
Norfolk	48
Suffolk	54
Essex	60
Kent	66
Sussex	72
Hampshire	78
Isle of Wight	84
Dorset	88
Channel Islands	96
Devon	100
Cornwall	108
Somerset & Gloucester	114
South Wales	120
West Wales	128
North Wales	134
Merseyside	140
Lancashire	146
Cumbria	152
Isle of Man	158
Southwest Scotland	162
Northwest Scotland	168
Northeast Scotland	174
Southeast Scotland	180
Index	186

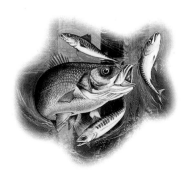

■ *This is a superb flounder mark which can produce quality fish all year. There are a number hot spots on either side of the river, but the most convenient and therefore most popular area is the walkway along the north bank.*

This walkway, from the bridge leading around towards the open sea, is an ideal venue for small pegged events. It provides a safe, fair and productive venue for youngsters.

SPECIES

Flounder to 2lb can be landed most months and eel will show from June through until October. The River Aln has a tremendous reputation, as a sea trout fishery and occasionally one of these is foul-hooked. Sea trout should be returned.

BEST BAITS

Fresh peeler crabs are best for flounder and eel. During colder months when crab is hard to obtain, worms tipped with mackerel strip or a sliver of sandeel will take plenty of fish.

TACKLE

Lightweight tackle is all that is required because the river is fairly narrow and a short lob is all that is needed to put your bait in the centre of the flow. Fish 18lb mainline all through, a two-hook trace and a 2oz rolling sinker. Most

match anglers use the fine-wire Mustad Nordic Bend 4446B hooks.

GETTING THERE

Take the A1068 north from Ashington and head for Alnmouth, passing Amble and Warkworth. At the Hipburn roundabout, bear right towards Alnmouth and the road crosses the bridge. Park up safely next to the bridge on the left-hand side of the road. The fishing marks are accessed via footpaths either side of the bridge.

TACKLE SHOPS

● *R L Jobson, Bondgate Within, Alnwick,*
Tel: 01665 602135.

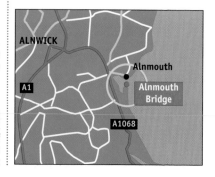

■ *This is cracking spot capable of producing some really outstanding sport when the fish are inshore in numbers.*

The shoreline in front of the village is protected by a series of rocky skeers, which lead to a small harbour and breakwater, to the south is a two-mile unbroken stretch of golden sands.

The rock edges have produced many outstanding catches of cod to double figures from the front skeers and the flat rocks behind the harbour. The breakwater can give good sport at high tide for coalies and mackerel, depending on the time of year. Flounder plus the occasional plaice, dab or turbot are caught along the sandy bay.

SPECIES
The main target will be cod, but coalfish, pollack, ballan wrasse, bass, flounder and eel also feature.

BEST BAITS
Use peeler crabs in summer. Lugworms take over in winter and can prove very effective when mixed with mussels, clams or razorfish. Crabs or worms tipped off with a sliver of mackerel will catch flatfish on the clean beach marks.

TACKLE
For rock-end fishing, use a 13ft beachcaster coupled with a Abu 7000-type multiplier reel, 30lb mainline, 60lb shockleader, a single-hook trace and 5oz wired sinker incorporating a rotten-bottom system.

For beach work, change to an Abu 6500-type reel with 15lb mainline, 40lb shockleader and multi-hook traces.

GETTING THERE
Take the B1339 from Embleton, turn right at Swinhoe onto the B1340 and head for Beadnell. You'll find there is plenty of parking space adjacent to the beach or along the seafront as you approach the village.

TACKLE SHOP
● *Amble Angling Centre, Newburgh St, Amble, Tel: 01665 711200.*

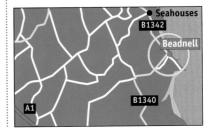

■ *The rocks edges are only fishable approximately two hours either side of low water, with the best catches taken from early autumn until the beginning of spring when cod shoals are pushed inshore by the easterly gales.*

Cambois rocks are a noted big-fish mark and a few cod of over 20lb are landed in most seasons, with sport peaking around the turn of the year.

On a big spring tide, when the full extent of the skeers are revealed, a network of deep weed-filled gullies are exposed. On these tides, a large peeler crab bait lobbed into the middle of a gully can often produce spectacular bites, which generally result in a nice plump cod being landed.

SPECIES
Cod and coalfish make up the bulk of fish landed from these rock edges. This is big-fish mark and fish to over 25lb are landed or lost most seasons.

BEST BAITS
Peeler crabs are very effective throughout the year. Lugworms, ragworms, white rag, squid and shellfish baits catch fish at various times through the year.

TACKLE
Use a 13ft beachcaster matched with a 7000-size multiplier reel, 35lb mainline straight through, a single hook trace, which should incorporate a rotten-bottom system, and a 5oz wired sinker.

GETTING THERE
Take the A189 north over the River Blyth, then the Cambois slip road heading for the sea front. Follow the second exit at the roundabout, drive past North Blyth and follow the road that runs along the side of the railway. Park adjacent to the Alcan factory entrance.

TACKLE SHOP
● *CD Tackle, 91 Front St, Newbiggin, Tel: 01670 520133.*

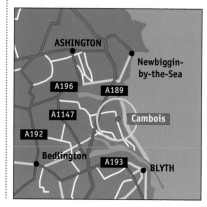

BOG HALL ROCKS
Lynemouth, Northumberland

■ *Situated at the north end of Lynemouth beach, this is a consistent area for winter cod during daylight or darkness.*

You can fish the rocks two hours either side of low water, but it is best as the sea is dying away.

On the big tides the water tends to be coloured. There are several spots to fish on Bog Hall rocks, depending on the state of tide. Normally, as soon as you get on, you can cast off the very front which is the part known as the High Side. Fish show straight away on the ebb. If nothing happens after the first hour, move south onto the lower skeers casting either east off the front or back towards Lynemouth beach. Both areas produce fish.

Another spot is on the North Corner, which can be fished on a big tide. There is a island which becomes exposed off the front off the Square Hole. If the sea is running from the south-east the front of Bog Hall becomes unfishable, but the Square Hole on the north side becomes a good mark. Short casting into the weedy Square Hole can produce some large fish when the sea conditions are good.

SPECIES
Cod are the target fish.

BEST BAITS
Use peeler crab bait from September to November, but worm baits come into there own in winter. Cocktail baits of lug and rag and mussels work well, but lug and white rag is best.

TACKLE
You will need strong tackle. Load a 7000-sized multiplier with 25lb-30lb mainline.

Keep rigs simple. A single hook or Pennell rig is normally used. Hooks are normally size 2/0-4/0 Mustad Vikings. It is advisable to use a rotten-bottom attachment on your sinkers.

When you strike into your fish, keep it moving because there are rocks and weed for your fish to dive into.

GETTING THERE
From the A1, turn off for Morpeth and Ashington. Take the A1068 towards Amble, turning off for Ellington and Lynemouth. The venue is situated at the north of Lynemouth beach, near Cresswell, so a walk is required. You can only get on the rocks at low water.

TACKLE SHOP
● *CD Fishing Tackle, 91 Front St, Newbiggin, Tel: 01670 520133.*

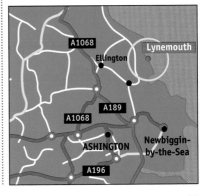

■ *The best areas to fish around Seahouses are from the rocky skeers below the south pier. This rough, kelpy ground produces excellent cod fishing throughout the summer and winter.*

Fish the gullies during a calm sea. Expect good results when the sea has flattened off after a blow. The bigger tides are usually more productive. Best times to fish are two hours down to low water and two hours back up.

SPECIES

Red codling, which feed among the kelp during summer, are joined by cleaner winter fish from November onwards.

BEST BAITS

A live peeler crab is the top summer bait, with July offering the chance to us live edible peelers, which are even more productive. A cocktail of worms and a frozen peeler works well during the winter.

TACKLE

Heavy gear, such as a stiff 13ft beachcaster and 7000-sized multiplier loaded with 35lb line straight through, is needed. Single size 4/0 hook rigs will give you the best chance of getting anything back through the kelp.

GETTING THERE

Seahouses is off the main A1. Leave the A1 on the B6347 or B1341 and join the B1340 road into Seahouses. Park around the harbour. Make sure you do not park in the caravan site to the south of the harbour.

TACKLE SHOP

● *R L Jobson, Bondgate Within, Alnwick, Tel: 01665 602135.*

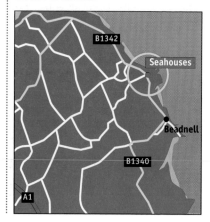

■ *This is an all-weather mark which can be fished in reasonable comfort in any conditions. The harbour is protected by an offshore reef about 200 yards from the shore and can offer spectacular sport when all other marks are unfishable.*

The heavier the sea the better the chance of quality fish. There is no time of the year when cod cannot be expect from this mark.

SPECIES
High tide during the summer will produce good bags of coalfish to 2lb, red cod to 5lb and wrasse to 4lb fishing from the rocks in front of the harbour.

Flounder to 2lb are caught from the sandy area of the harbour.

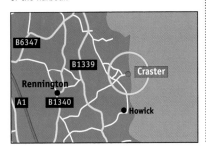

This area produces cod into double-figures and coalfish to 3lb from late August until March.

BEST BAITS
Fresh peeler crabs are the only bait worth using in summer, but as the weather cools then frozen crabs and lugworms tipped with razorfish or mussels are effective.

TACKLE
The heavy nature of the bottom means that you have to use a 7000-type reel with at least 30lb line and a single hook rotten-bottom rig for cod, coalfish and ballan wrasse.

A normal two or three-hook match rig can be used when fishing within the harbour for flounders.

GETTING THERE
Take the B1339 for Embleton. Just after Longhoughton take the Howick road, which takes you along the cliff top past Cullernose Point. Half a mile further, turn right for Craster. There is plenty of parking within five minutes of the venue.

TACKLE SHOP
● *R L Jobson, Bondgate Within, Alnwick, Tel: 01665 602135.*

15

THE BLACK MIDDENS
Tynemouth, Tyne & Wear

■ The Middens are a massive rock formation on the north bank of the Tyne, jutting out some distance into the harbour area.

They are accessible over low water with best catches taken during the big spring tides, when a cast of 100 yards will put your bait into the main channel.

The Tyne can produce good catches of cod throughout the year and is never unfishable. The marks are surrounded by sand, mud, mussel beds, shingle and weedy patches.

SPECIES
Expect good bags of coalies and codling in winter when other marks struggle to perform. Flounder are the main quarry in September and October, especially on spring tides.

BEST BAITS
Peeler crabs are best. Lugworms, ragworms and fish strips are effective in winter.

TACKLE
Use a medium-weight beachcaster coupled with a 7000-type multiplier reel, 30lb mainline, 60lb shockleader, a two-hook trace and a 5oz breakout sinker.

Chest waders are definitely necessary as the tide does creep in behind you, so a quick exit may be required.

GETTING THERE
Take the A19 north through the Tyne Tunnel and then turn right onto the A193 east heading for North Shields. Once there, drive through the town centre until you reach the outskirts of Tynemouth. The Middens are situated on the north side of the harbour.

Parking is available at the bottom of Tanners Bank or adjacent to Knott's Flats, or even in the Collingwood Memorial car park.

TACKLE SHOP
● *Steve's Tackle, Prudhoe St, North Shields, Tel: 0191 257 9999.*

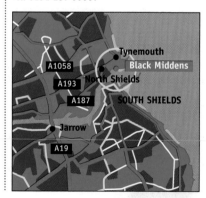

16

■ *The harbour and surrounding rock edges are a mix of offshore islands, deep gullies and rocky skeers. The majority of action takes place over low water, when the full extent of weed-covered boulders are exposed.*

To the north, Crab Hill Island offers the opportunity of reaching further out even when the sea is really rough. Moving south, you find the Warrior Gut, The Mary's, Goat's Gully, The Nancy's and then the harbour skeers.

On the south side of the harbour, the top skeer is the hot spot when the northerly seas are raging. The best advice is to put your bait into the middle of a gully.

SPECIES
Cod are the most prolific species, followed closely by coalfish and rockling, with the autumn bringing silver eel. A number of conger have been hooked, but not landed.

BEST BAITS
Peeler crabs are best throughout the year. Lugworms, ragworms and most shellfish are effective and often used as a cocktail, tipping with peeler.

TACKLE
The area is one large weed bed with prolific kelp-beds, so use a 13 ft beachcaster coupled with an 7000-type reel, 35lb mainline all through, a single hook trace with a 5oz wired sinker incorporating a rotten-bottom system.

GETTING THERE
Take the A1058 east coast road from Newcastle and head for Tynemouth. Go straight ahead at the Broadway pub roundabout until you reach the sea front. Turn left, following the coast north for approximately half a mile and you arrive at Cullercoats harbour. Parking is allowed at a number of designated areas.

TACKLE SHOP
● *Steve's Tackle, Prudhoe St, North Shields, Tel: 0191 257 9999.*

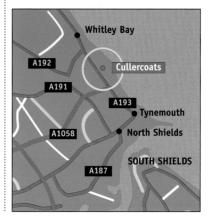

■ *This popular area on the south side of the River Tyne produces good bags of coalfish, codling and flounder during the autumn.*

The sea bed is a mixture of mud and shingle and the water is very deep close in. There are a few snags. Overcast days produce well, otherwise you are better off fishing at night either side of low water.

SPECIES

Autumn and winter produce good bags of coalfish and cod to 9lb, with good quality flounder featuring in catches.

May marks the start of the flounder action

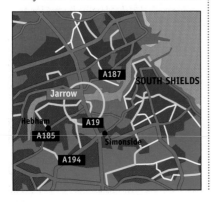

followed by eel, codling and a few coalfish. Sport can be slow when there is a lot of cold floodwater in the river.

BEST BAITS

Peeler crabs produce eel and flounder in summer, while the codling and coalfish prefer ragworms.

TACKLE

Standard beach fishing gear is all you will need short casting is all that is required, a 50 yard lob will do. You will need grip leads to combat the tide and three-hook flapping rig with size 2 hooks covers all options during the summer.

It is advisable to use a single size 2/0 hook paternoster for the codling during the winter. You will need to use a drop-net to land the bigger codling, so make sure you go prepared.

Try fishing one rod down the side of the wall, where you can pick up some good eel and flounder.

GETTING THERE

Jarrow can be found on the south side of the river just west of the Tyne tunnel. There is a car park with a path that leads to the promenade.

TACKLE SHOP

● *ID Fishing, 206 Ocean Rd, South Shields, Tel: 0191 455 3022.*

■ St Mary's Island, which is also known as Bait Island, is the most easily recognised mark in Whitley Bay.

The north side of the island fishes best and Crisp Gully is well worth a try.

This is a low-water mark and the last two hours of the ebb and first two hours of the flood produce the best results. The sea bed consists of rocks and kelp and anglers are forced to use strong gear. However, there are one or two clear patches about 60 to 70 yards out. Avoid the area during rough weather.

SPECIES
In summer, anglers can expect a few codling, coalfish and wrasse, while coalfish and codling, sometimes reaching double-figure weights, are caught in winter. The best catches often come between October and January.

BEST BAITS
Crabs, either fresh or frozen, are best, but mussels, lugworms and ragworms are worth trying.

TACKLE
Most local fishermen use strong 13ft beach rods with 7000-size reels and 25lb to 30lb mainline. Rigs are a single hook on a 3ft flowing trace about 2ft above a 6oz grip lead. Use a size 3/0 to 4/0 hook and then try casting between 80 and 100 yards out.

GETTING THERE
Take the A193 out of Whitley Bay following signs for Seaton. Signs for St Mary's are off to the right. A causeway, which is covered by water on the last couple of hours of the flood, links the island to the mainland. A car park can be found close by on the mainland.

TACKLE SHOP
● *Steve's Tackle, Prudhoe St, North Shields, Tel: 0191 257 9999.*

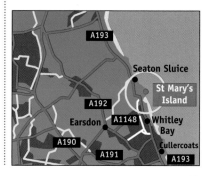

19

■ *The River Wear is an amazing fishery that seems to fish its head off when everywhere else is struggling for form. The marks at South Hylton, next to the Golden Lion Pub, nestled under the A19 flyover, are no exception.*

Summer eel fishing can produce non-stop action, just as the evening light is starting to fade. Sport has held up very well, despite the large number of flounder caught every season.

SPECIES
Flounder are present throughout the year, although local clubs tend to fish these marks only during the summer. Eels are caught during the summer. Coalfish and sea trout are occasional catches.

BEST BAITS
Peeler crabs are essential in summer. At other times, you will need to have a good variety of baits. Runnidown lugworms can be deadly, as can white rag, kippers, shelled prawns and mackerel strip.

TACKLE
Most types of tackle can be seen in action on these popular marks, from junior spinning outfits to heavy beachcasting gear. Match anglers use light rods coupled with an 6500-type multiplier or a bass/carp rod coupled with a Shimano Baitrunner-type fixed-spool reel.

A two-hook trace using fine-wire hooks and a sinker to match the tide run are usually successful.

GETTING THERE
Take the A19 from the Tyne Tunnel and head south. Drive past the Nissan factory to the right. Cross over the River Wear and take the next slip road signposted Sunderland South onto the A183. At the first roundabout turn left for Pennywell and then left again approximately one mile further heading for South Hylton. This road will take you to the riverside next to the Golden Lion Pub.

TACKLE SHOP
● *Rutherford's Tackle, 125 Roker Ave, Sunderland, Tel: 0191 565 4183.*

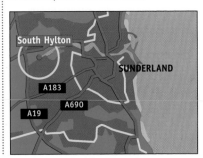

■ *This is an excellent autumn and winter venue for codling and coalfish. The ground can be extremely rough around low water when rocky outcrops and kelp-infested gullies become home to the fish.*

Three hours before low water and one hour into the flood fishes best. Daylight fishes well when the water is coloured and there is a heavy swell. Night produces the best results.

Fish the north end of Whitley Bay beach during a heavy-swell. Fish from the south end when the swell is moderate.

BEST BAITS
The first run of fish early in September are preoccupied with peeler crabs, but from November through to April, a number of different baits will catch. Try using lugworms, ragworms, mussels, white ragworms and frozen crabs. Mussels and frozen peeler crab cocktails can be deadly.

TACKLE
Due to the nature of the sea bed, most anglers use a stiff rod with a 7000-sized multiplier loaded with 35lb mainline and no shockleader.

Single-hook rigs between sizes 2/0 and 4/0 are standard with snoods made from 30-35lb mono. A breakout-style lead of 5oz-6oz is ample to hold bottom.

GETTING THERE
Take the A193 coast road and park opposite the swimming baths where Whitley Bay AC headquarters can be found.

TACKLE SHOP
● *Temple's Tackle, 43 Ocean View, Whitley Bay, Tel: 0191 252 6017.*

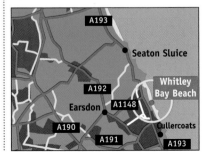

21

■ *The Blackhall Colliery beach and rock edges provide anglers with superb ranges of fishing marks capable of producing tremendous bags of fish throughout the year.*

Although codling to 4lb are the mainstay, fish to double figures are a real possibility, with plenty of whiting, coalfish and even the occasional school bass. Now that coal dumping has ceased,

and the water is clearer, night fishing is the prime time when the beach comes to life and only a slight swell is required to coax the fish inshore, within casting distance. Anglers should be aware that there are plenty of snags, just waiting to foul-hook your end gear, so it pays to use heavy line and a rotten bottom sinker system.

SPECIES
The rock edges yield a mixture of cod, coalfish, eel, whiting and the occasional bass. The sandy areas to the north produce flounder, plaice. dabs and again plenty of whiting.

BEST BAITS
During the summer peeler crabs take some beating, but as the weather cools black runnidown lug takes over as the top bait. Tipping lugworm baits with silvers (white rag) or mackerel strip will increase your catch.

TACKLE
Fishing this type of mark can often result in heavy tackle loses, so the best advice is to err on the heavy side, thereby making sure any fish hooked is safely landed.

Use a good quality beachcaster, such as a Cono-flex Armageddon, coupled with an Abu 7000-type multiplier reel, 35lb mainline all through and a single hook trace incorporating a rotten-bottom system with a 6oz wired sinker.

GETTING THERE
Take the A19 south past Seaham and Easington and turn left at the Peterlee junction. Drive through Peterlee and turn right at Horden onto the A1086 heading for Blackhall Colliery. As you drive through the village, turn left adjacent to the local chippie, aptly named 'The Plaice', and follow the road down towards the seafront.

The fishing marks are only a short walk away with the rock edges, known as the Caves to the south and the beach to the north.

TACKLE SHOP
● *Coast Road Tackle, Sunderland Rd, Horden, Tel: 0191 518 0742.*

■ *The Durham Colliery beaches have undergone a dramatic change and there have been great improvements to the general environment in the effort to erase the industrial scars of the past. During the 1980s at Easington Flight, where coal waste was deposited into the sea 24 hours a day, the water was black and as a consequence fishing was excellent regardless of the time of day.*

The general clean up following the cessation of coal dumping has affected sport to the extent that as the water is much clearer the fish population now includes lots of species that are new to the area.

During the autumn and winter, the beach can definitely be relied upon to produce some outstanding catches of codling, coalfish and whiting. If a good swell is running the Fox Holes, at the south end of the beach, is the big-fish hot spot, capable of throwing up a few double figured cod most seasons.

SPECIES
Cod and coalfish are the main quarry with flounder and dab taken from the cleaner stretches of the beach. The last couple of seasons have seen the whiting population increase and it has been difficult to avoid these scavenging marauders, who seem intent upon taking any bait offered.

BEST BAITS
The top bait, which will catch fish throughout the year, is runnidown lugworms, often tipped off with either white rag or, if whiting are about, a sliver of mackerel. Fresh peeler crabs in

season can be deadly, especially when eel are showing during the autumn.

TACKLE
The area is liberally sprinkled with patches of rough ground, so it will pay to use a strong beachcaster, such as a Cono-flex Armageddon, coupled with Abu 6500-type multiplier, 25lb mainline, 50lb shockleader, a two-hook trace and a 6oz breakout sinker. Use good quality hooks, such as Mustad Vikings.

GETTING THERE
Take the A19 south past Seaham and, at the next junction, fork left onto the Sunderland road. At Easington village, turn left onto the B1283 and head for Easington Colliery. As the B1283 turns south at the outskirts of village, head for Horden parking opposite the row of terraced houses in Office Street. The marks are a good 10-minute walk away down the Grand Canyon, which is a wide steep track, leading directly to the beach.

TACKLE SHOPS
● **Rigs Tackle Shop, 72 Church St, Seaham, Tel: 0191 581 7915.**
● **Coast Road Tackle, 3 Sunderland Rd, Horden, Tel: 0191 518 0742.**

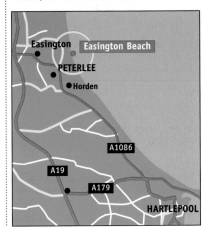

■ *This is a large expanse of sand swept by fierce tides, which at times form big sandbars with large, deep holes in between. It is essentially a low water mark that fishes best during daylight. Crimdon can change from one tide to the next, so it is essential to take a look in daylight at low water to see where the holes have formed. On the big spring low tides, it is possible to get onto the far sandbar and fish a few hours either side of low water, but usually you are restricted to fishing the middle hole, usually called the Clay Hole.*

The beach will produce some fish in most conditions, except when there is a south-easterly wind blowing.

SPECIES
Mixed bags of up to 30 codling and whiting are not uncommon, with the codling averaging 3lb. September to March is the best time for codling and whiting, though it will fish in the summer if there is a sea running.

BEST BAITS
Fresh worm baits are the best option with very few fish taking crabs. Tipping off with mackerel will take whiting to 2lb.

TACKLE
Use a standard beach rod and 6500-size multiplier. A 30-yard cast into a hole is all that is needed. Calmer conditions mean it is possible to fish with a bass or carp rod. Bites can be ferocious, almost pulling the rod from its rest.

GETTING THERE
Parking your vehicle here can be dangerous as it is plagued by car thieves at night. The best option is to park at Parton and walk along the beach or to park behind the Steeley factory on the main road and access the beach through a tunnel under the railway line.

TACKLE SHOPS
● *Anglers Services, 27 Park Rd, Hartlepool, Tel: 01429 274844.*
● *Cairns Angling, Mainsforth Terrace, Hartlepool, Tel: 01429 272581.*
● *John F Gent, 161 York Rd, Hartlepool, Tel: 01429 272585.*

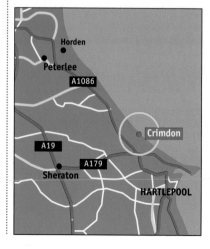

■ The Chemical Beach is one of the outstanding areas on this coast and is located just south of Seaham harbour and north of Blast Beach and Hawthorn Point.

There is a fairly steep slope on this beach at high water and the sea bed is reasonably clean. However, it can be scoured out by big seas, revealing bare rock which can lead to heavy tackle losses at times.

In the past it was the acidic liquid from the coal-washing process, brought by tankers and poured onto the Chemical Beach, that gave the area its name.

Best time to fish is after a decent blow, when there is a good swell running. There should be excellent catches of codling for anglers fishing at all distances from close to as far as you are able to cast.

As the wind dies down and the swell leaves the water, the fish will usually move out and distance casting pays off. Whiting appear in better numbers as the sea becomes calmer. Cold, frosty nights seem to encourage more fish to feed.

SPECIES
Main species are codling and whiting, but plaice, coalfish and dogfish also feature.

BEST BAITS
Main choices are lugworms and black lug, especially tipped with white rag, which catch codling and whiting. Peeler crabs and mussels work for codling, while rag will catch codling and whiting. Fish baits and black lug will work to catch whiting.

TACKLE
Use one or two-hook rigs with a long, trailing hook or a one-up, one-down combination. Rigs can be clipped down for distance. Hook size depends on bait and species. Use a size 1 or 1/0 for small whiting, but a size 1/0-4/0 for codling and anything larger. You will need some 5oz or 6oz plain or grip leads.

GETTING THERE
Take the A19 south from Sunderland past Seaham. At Cold Hesledon, turn left onto the A182 and head east for the coast. Just after the third roundabout it is possible to drive over a rough track and park near Nose's Point. The Chemical beach is then just a short walk down the cliffs paths.

TACKLE SHOP
● Rigs Tackle Shop, 72 Church St, Seaham, Tel: 0191 581 7272.

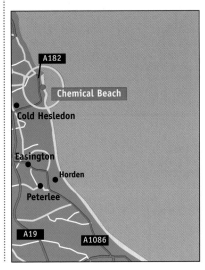

■ *Once as famous as Chesil Beach in Dorset, the Blast is still one of the most productive shore marks in the country.*

In recent years the end of coal dumping and general clean up has severely affected the cod fishing. Cleaner water and a reduction in pollution have resulted in a big decline in cod catches, but vastly improved whiting and flatfish sport has more than balanced this out.

Many local anglers consider the beach to be a long distance casting venue and the person who can put a lead well over the 100-yard mark generally takes the biggest catches.

At night, when the fish venture closer to the shore, distance casting is no advantage.

SPECIES
During the winter, codling can be landed in good numbers, if they can outwit the vast whiting shoals intent upon devouring any bait offered. Other species include coalfish, rockling and in the summer small bass and dogfish.

BEST BAITS
Most types of worms will take fish, although runnidown lugworms and snake whites are considered the premier baits. During the autumn, whiting seem to prefer plain worm baits, with lug and rag often taking most of the fish. As the waters cool, fish baits take over.

TACKLE
Use a good quality long distance casting rod coupled with a 6500-type multiplier, 15lb mainline, 50lb shockleader, a two-hook clipped down rig and a 6oz breakout sinker. For general fishing at night, use a three-hook flapper rig with two-up and one-down.

GETTING THERE
Take the A19 south from Sunderland past Seaham, at Cold Hesledon turn left onto the A182 and head east for the coast. Just after the second roundabout, park carefully at the roadside. The Blast Beach stretches off to the south for approximately two miles.

TACKLE SHOP
● *Rigs Tackle Shop, 72 Church St, Seaham, Tel: 0191 581 7272.*

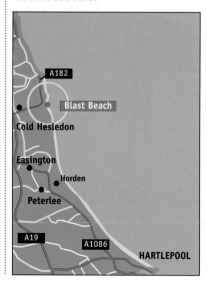

■ This is a popular match venue on one of County Durham's popular former colliery beaches. It has some rocky patches.

It fishes best for two hours either side of high water and the last three hours of the flood up to high water. Best results come on a dying sea after rough weather. A good north-west wind will put a good sea onto the beach, while a southerly wind is considered a waste of time.

It was the dumped coal waste that turned the local beaches black; it is estimated that 15,000 tons of waste were tipped into the sea every week from the Blast tip. Now winter storms have removed the coal dust.

The Seaham club organise matches in this area and their events in the 1970s regularly attracted several thousand anglers.

SPECIES

Expect to catch codling and whiting from late August to February, odd flounder and plaice, along with coalfish and dogfish.

BEST BAITS

Black lugworms and white rag catch codling, but mussels and clams produce fish. Peeler crabs work for summer codling. Autumn whiting like worm baits, tipped off with mackerel or sandeel.

TACKLE

Use a 13ft beachcaster and a reel loaded with 15lb-25lb mainline and 50lb shockleader. Two and sometimes three-hooks clipped-down carrying size 1/0 to 3/0 hooks are best. Long casts can be useful at times.

GETTING THERE

Horden is south of Seaham and due east of Peterlee.

TACKLE SHOP

● *Coast Road Tackle, 3 Sunderland Rd, Horden, Tel: 0191 518 0742.*

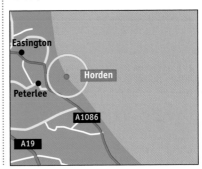

from about half-tide, depending on the size of the tide and how rough the sea is. Some more experienced anglers, who know the area well, can get cut off and fish over high water, as the cod will run out of the kelp and up the scars when the water is coloured.

This area is notorious for its big fish. In recent years plenty of double-figure fish up to 17lb have been caught. With this mark being so exposed, it doesn't want a big sea and will often produce fish in calm conditions when there is plenty of colour in the water.

SPECIES

Mainly cod, with a few smaller species, such as rockling, pouting and coalfish. Don't be surprised to get the occasional bass.

■ Located on most maps as Hummersea Scar, this northerly-facing mark nestles between Boulby and Skinningrove on boundary of the Yorkshire and Cleveland coast.

This is mainly a low water mark, when anglers can probe the kelp-fringed holes that are exposed as the tide ebbs out. Fishing is best from October through to March, traditionally winter fishing.

The most popular mark is the old harbour, which can produce good bags of fish, as you can fish it several hours either side of low water. Anglers must be wary as there is a cut-off here

BEST BAITS

For cod, undoubtedly the top bait is a fresh crab when available. However, a frozen crab is just as good most times. Worms and mussels will catch fish, especially when used as cocktail baits with a crab.

TACKLE

This is a no frills venue, so it is standard rough ground tackle of a 13ft rock rod with a 7000-size reel loaded with 30lb line and a shockleader. The terminal tackle is usually a 5oz-6oz plain lead, rigged for rotten bottom use, with a 4/0-6/0 hook depending on personal preference. Grip leads can be useful if the sea is heavy enough to keep moving the tackle out of the fishing area.

GETTING THERE

Take the A174 Whitby-Saltburn road and access is via a small road linking Boulby with Loftus and parallel to the A174. Follow this down the steep hill and turn right. Parking is very limited and don't block access to farmland. A small path leads to the beach and from here head south towards the high cliffs.

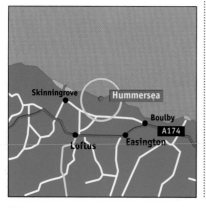

TACKLE SHOP

● **Keith's Sports, 31 Milton St, Saltburn, Tel: 01287 624296.**

■ This Victorian pier, which was re-opened in July 2001, has been significantly shortened over the years due to shipping disasters and heavy seas. It currently stretches 300 yards into the sea.

Codling and whiting sport starts around September and runs through to April. Fish two hours either side of high water for best results with the start of the ebb usually best. Always try to fish in darkness with a slight northerly or south-easterly sea condition prevailing.

There are no restrictions or charges, with fishing all the way up the pier on both sides when depth of water permits it.

SPECIES
The pier produces excellent bags of codling, whiting, dab and bass.

BEST BAITS
Lugworms and ragworms tipped with squid, fish or white ragworms take the most fish. When seas are very rough, crabs and mussels catch codling.

TACKLE
Most of the fishing is on to clean sand, except from the end of the pier where small snags from old pier pylons can be encountered.

Simple tactics of either one, two or three hook paternoster rigs are all that is required. A normal beach set-up capable of casting 50 yards is all you need. Hooks should be no larger than size 2/0 because the venue is not noted for its huge cod.

If the sea is not too heavy, move away from the end of the pier and cast close to the shore behind the breakers.

GETTING THERE
From the A19 pick up the A174 to Redcar, Guisborough and Whitby. Follow this road to Saltburn and continue towards Whitby, which takes you down a steep bank towards the shore. The pier will be on your left at the bottom of the bank, where there is a large car park.

TACKLE SHOP
● *Keith's Sports, 31 Milton St, Saltburn, Tel: 01287 624296.*

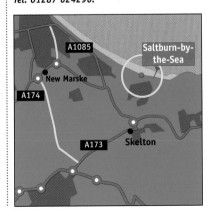

THE HEUGH
Hartlepool, Cleveland

coalfish. Lugworms and white rag also have their day. Try cocktails of a peeler crab, squid, worms and mackerel. Experimenting with different baits often brings surprising results.

TACKLE
A simple three-hook rig with size 1/0 or 2/0 hooks will cope with most of the fish you are likely to catch.

GETTING THERE
Take the A689 East from the A1 to Hartlepool. The piers are clearly signposted along the sea front.

TACKLE SHOPS
● *Anglers Services, 27 Park Rd, Hartlepool, Tel: 01429 274844.*
● *Flynn's Fishing Tackle & Country Wear, 12 Varo Terrace, Stockton-on-Tees, Tel: 01642 676473.*

■ *The Heugh breakwater (pronounced Huff) is supposedly the most productive pier in the whole of the North-East.*

The ground in front of the breakwater is a mixture of sand and rock patches situated in deep water. There is a barrier on this mark to prevent access, although it is still fished by many anglers, but be warned.

The nearby rocks, which are visible between the Heugh and the Pilot pier, also give good sport, this is extremely rough ground requiring a rotten-bottom rig.

Fish two hours either side of high water for best results on the breakwater, two hours either side of low water if you are fishing the rocks. It doesn't really make much difference whether the sea is rough or calm due to the depth of water.

SPECIES
Mainly codling and coalfish. Fishing down the side accounts for the most coalfish.

BEST BAITS
Peeler crabs works well for both the cod and

30

■ *When fishing from this promenade mark at high water, the ground directly in front is sandy. However, as the tide ebbs away to low water, patches of rock become visible and give way gradually to rougher ground and weed.*

Rough conditions from September to April give the best fishing, especially after dark. Two hours either side of high water is best from the promenade. Two hours either side of low water is best from the rocks. Spring tides fish best.

SPECIES
Codling, whiting, coalfish, flounder and occasional bass.

BEST BAITS
Yellowtail lugworms tipped with white rag on a clipped-down rig cast 100 yards at high water in rough weather is best. Lug and rag are popular over high water, but yellowtails with white rag will out-fish anything. Fresh or frozen crabs and mussels are the best low water baits.

TACKLE
Use a clipped-down paternoster rig from the promenade at high water. Size 2/0 and 3/0 hooks are ideal.

At low water, a one-hook paternoster will reduce tackle loss, especially if a rotten-bottom link is incorporated. Use 18lb mainline at high water, but the low water mark will need at least 25lb mainline to combat the snags.

GETTING THERE
Take the A689 east from the A1 to Hartlepool. Follow the signs for Seaton Carew and then for the sea front. The Staincliffe Hotel overlooks the sea going towards Hartlepool.

TACKLE SHOPS
● *Anglers Services, 27 Park Rd, Hartlepool, Tel: 01429 274844.*
● *Flynn's Fishing Tackle & Country Wear, 12 Varo Terrace, Stockton-on-Tees, Tel: 01642 676473.*

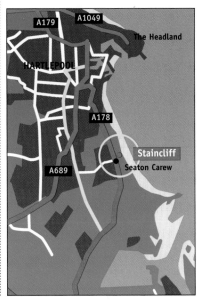

■ *This venue produces amazing bags of fish in a very short period of time, with 15 or 20 fish in a session considered normal.*

Access is very restricted and can only be gained on spring tides one-and-a-quarter hours either side of low water.

Safety is important here, so obtain local knowledge and fish with a local for a first session. Always have a watch with you and make sure you have the right tide times.

SPECIES
Main target species are coalfish, codling, eel, rockling and flounder. October to March produces good catches of codling and coalfish in darkness, when there is a north-easterly swell. Summer sport is for similar species.

BEST BAITS
Fresh crabs take some beating early in the year. Ragworms or a crab and mussels cocktail are best in winter.

TACKLE
Fishing is from a flat, mussel-covered scaur, casting a short distance into deep, kelp-filled gullies on either side.

A sturdy set-up is needed, with a strong beachcaster and 7000-sized multiplier loaded with 30lb mainline. Use either a 5oz plain or grip lead, depending on sea conditions. Use a single size 1/0 to 3/0 hook rig to avoid getting caught in the kelp.

GETTING THERE
Go along the A19 to the A174 junction to Whitby and Redcar. Follow the signs to Redcar and Teesside past the ICI complex, then follow the signs to Redcar. Take the road to the sea front and drive along the promenade to the end of the amusements.

Park on the main road in front of the fish boats at the end of the promenade. Walk down the last set of steps, near the pedestrian crossing, and the East Scaur is in front of you.

TACKLE SHOP
● *Redcar Angling Centre, 16 York Rd, Redcar, Tel: 01642 477106.*

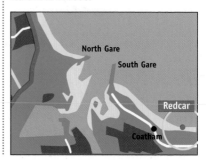

■ *These breakwaters at the entrance to the River Tees produce codling from October to March, in an easterly or north-easterly sea.*

Take care on the North Gare during big tides, if there is any movement on the sea, because the waves wash along its length. A moderate sea gives the best fishing. Avoid the right-hand corner because you will lose tackle every cast.

The South Gare is popular all year and suitable for junior and disabled anglers. Avoid the pier end in rough conditions. Coalfish are taken off the end in summer. Expect tackle losses at the right-hand side at the end. Fishing off the front and into the left-hand channel is for codling, whiting, and flatfish, but requires a good cast.

Large bags of mackerel can be expected from both piers during June to September.

SPECIES
Codling, whiting, coalfish, mackerel, bass, mullet and flatfish.

BEST BAITS
Ragworms and lugworms will take fish at most times, but crabs catch fish, especially off the left-hand corner of the North Gare. Float-fished mackerel strip or sprat tempts mackerel.

TACKLE
Standard beachcasting tackle will suffice at most times, but a good 6oz grip lead may be needed on bigger tides. A good cast is needed to clear

the rocks along the side of the North Gare and the end on the left side can be quite snaggy.

From the South Gare, try spinning, feathering or bottom fishing with a strip of mackerel attached to a small cork to keep it clear of the bottom. Float fishing is possible when it is not too crowded.

GETTING THERE
Access to the north and south banks of the River Tees is from the main A19, which passes through Middlesbrough. Use the A1046 and A178 for the north side.

For the south bank, take the A66 to Redcar and then follow the signs to Coatham and Warrenby, going through the steelworks.

TACKLE SHOPS
● *Anglers Services, 27 Park Rd, Hartlepool, Tel: 01429 274844.*
● *Flynn's Fishing Tackle & Country Wear, 12 Varo Terrace, Stockton-on-Tees, Tel: 01642 676473.*

■ Whiting and cod are the main quarry in autumn and winter at Atwick (pronounced Attic), which is two miles north of Hornsea on the coast road to Bridlington.

Good casting ability can be an advantage when the sea is flat, but is not necessary in rougher conditions. Locate the holes and banks and you can expect to catch fish.

Local anglers used to say fish the rocks until Christmas and the beaches after, but changes in recent years have seen this coastline produce cod from October.

The water is often coloured, so daylight and night sessions produce fish. Best times are two hours up to high water and two hours down,

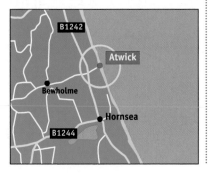

although low water fishing can be good if you are a good caster.

SPECIES
Cod and whiting, but in summer you will catch a few flounder, bass and eel.

BEST BAITS
Use lugworm for codling and whiting. Flounder, bass and eel respond to peeler crab and ragworm.

TACKLE
This is a sand beach offering clean ground fishing, so your tackle can be standard beach gear with a reel loaded with 15lb line. Use a 150g weight and 50lb shockleader.

GETTING THERE
Atwick is approached from either Bridlington or Hornsea on the B1242 coast road, or by turning off the A165 at Brandesburton and taking the minor road. Access can be difficult due to coastal erosion, but there is a track down to the beach. It is not suitable for disabled access.

TACKLE SHOP
● *East Coast Tackle, 1b Willow Dr, Hornsea,*
Tel: 01964 535064.

■ *A northerly-facing mark surrounded by low cliffs, it fishes best during the later part of winter. This venue has a very small tidal range and low water marks can be reached at high tide, giving the angler the ability to fish through the tide without having to move far.*

Most marks here are to the right of the car park, and fish best with sea on. Best times to fish are the flood up to high water. It can produce excellent fishing when a big south-easterly is running.

The rocks and ledges running from the back of the wyke are popular marks; the ground is fairly clean here. Ragglescar is prominent at the end of the wyke, and can produce fish over low water in calm conditions. The ground is extremely rough. To the left of the car park, marks produce good fishing in late summer, fishing into thick kelp.

SPECIES
Cod, cod, and more cod. However, in summer the wyke can produce good sport spinning for mackerel. Marks to the left of the wyke will also produce wrasse in summer.

BEST BAITS
Like most areas around here, fresh crabs are best. Most baits will take fish in winter, with mussels fishing well when the weather is particularly hard.

TACKLE
Standard cod tackle is the order of the day; a 13ft rock rod, 7000-size reel loaded with 30lb line, 60lb shockleader. Hooks are size 5/0-6/0 and plain 5-6oz leads are the norm.

GETTING THERE
Located five miles north of Scarborough on the A171 is Cloughton village. Take the small turn off by the Cober Hill guesthouse, located at the junction with the Ravenscar road. Follow this small road down to the coast where you will find a small parking area.

This public road runs through farmland, so please close the gates after you. Access to the rocks is located either straight down a grassy path from the parking area. For marks further along to the south of the wyke, follow the cliff top path for 400 yards until wooden steps are located and follow these down to the shore.

TACKLE SHOPS
● *Castle Foot Tackle, 1 Quay St, Scarborough, Tel: 01723 370390.*
● *GB Angling, 119 Victoria Rd, Scarborough, Tel: 01723 365000.*

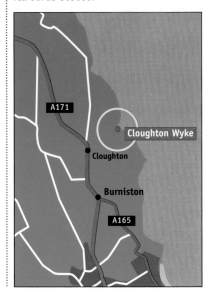

■ *This is a Humber estuary mark for all states of the tide with flounder on offer for most of the year. Good numbers of codling have been caught here in recent seasons. Fishing either side of low water is best.*

BEST BAITS

Crabs, lugworms, harbour rag, king rag and garden worms can be used for bait in summer, but lug and harbour rag are the best choices to use in winter.

TACKLE

You will require a standard beach rod and reel. Fish a two-up, one-down flapping rig at close range while the tide is running, but as the run eases you should cast a bit further. Use size 2 hooks in summer, stepping up to size 1 or 1/0 in winter. Use 30lb line straight through because there are a few snags.

GETTING THERE

Take the A63 towards Hull and go under the Humber Bridge. Take the second junction to the roundabout and the third exit, then right towards the Makro store. Fish along the wall behind it.

TACKLE SHOPS

● *The Fishing Basket, 470 Beverley Rd, Hull, Tel: 01482 445284.*
● *Chapman's Sea & Game, 21-29 Beechway, Ashby, Scunthorpe, Tel: 01724 270096.*

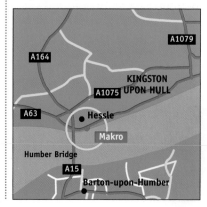

■ *This is one of the most versatile marks on the Yorkshire coast and fishes best from September through to March.*

The main Saltwick Hole, located in the middle of the bay, fishes best at low water with a good sea running, but fish can be taken at high tide from the beach at the back. Rock ledges either side of this are fished at low water, when conditions are calmer. Flat scaurs to the north do fish well throughout the tide, but fishing is best in the darkness.

SPECIES

Main species are cod, with double-figure fish taken most years. The flat scaurs to the north produce quality flounder and coalfish in September, and occasional eel. Expect odd school bass from the beach towards the south of the hole.

BEST BAITS

Top bait is a fresh crab especially for cod, flounder and eel. Later in the year frozen crabs, lug, and mussels will all take fish, especially cocktail baits.

TACKLE

Not really a place for light tackle, so most anglers use a 13ft rock rod with a 7000-size reel. Mainline is around 30lb with a 60lb shockleader. In most marks a 5oz plain lead is used, but on the flat scaurs it often pays to use a grip lead. Hooks are mainly size 5/0-6/0 forged, enough to present a good-sized bait and hold a good fish. However, if fishing the flat scaurs, two 1/0-2/0 hooks are useful for the flounder and coalfish, but strong enough to handle a cod.

GETTING THERE

Take the A171 south of Whitby or North from Scarborough, and Saltwick is located just of this road a mile south of Whitby. Access this mark through a road that leads to a caravan site, just south of Whitby Abbey. Park on the grass verge located outside the camp. Access to the beach is via a path that leads from the cliff top.

TACKLE SHOP

● *Whitby Angling Supplies, 65 Haggersgate, Whitby, Tel: 01947 603855.*

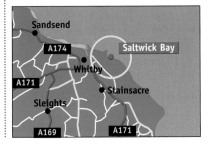

■ *This is a venue that doesn't need a lot of sea to produce fish. Some of the best fishing can be had towards the end of summer, when the sea is flat and clear.*

Optimum time to fish is two hours either side of low water on spring tides, which gives anglers the opportunity to pick out the holes dotted among the thick bands of kelp.

In summer, cod take on a red colour to blend in with the kelp and are locally known as natives. Most of the shore is a mixture of boulders and kelp, it often pays to have a cast then move until a pocket of fish is located, as these fish are territorial and don't shoal.

Fish can be caught all year, but good fishing can be had in winter and during choppy easterly seas that put some colour in the water, but not much movement can produce the goods. This venue is unfishable in big seas.

SPECIES
Really an out and out cod venue, but good wrasse to 4lb can be plentiful in summer.

TACKLE
This is heavy ground, so a rod with plenty of backbone is required to haul fish from the kelp, a typical 13ft heavy ground rod should suit.

Reels should be 7000 or 9000-size loaded with 30lb line and a shockleader.

Leads are plain 5oz-6oz fitted with rotten-bottom rigs, while hooks should be size 5/0-6/0 forged, attached to 35lb snood.

BEST BAITS
Fresh peeler crabs, especially edible and velvets, are the top baits in summer. In winter, frozen crabs are best and especially fished as cocktails.

GETTING THERE
Located seven miles north of Scarborough, take the Ravenscar road off the A171 at Cloughton. Then after a mile take the right turning down to the Hayburn Wyke Hotel and use the car park (there may be a small charge).

Follow the track through the woods down to the shore and then head north around the small headland at Hayburn Wyke. There isn't anything obvious to Staintondale, but after about 20 minutes walk you should be in the right vicinity.

TACKLE SHOP
● *Castle Foot Tackle, 1 Quay St, Scarborough, Tel: 01723 370390.*

HAYBURN WYKE
Scarborough, Yorkshire

■ *This is a scenic bay facing north with a backdrop of cliffs, where fish tend to average 3lb-5lb.*

It has two distinct peak times to fish. Firstly mid to late summer, with gin-clear water during daylight and dead calm seas, is the best time to tempt red cod from the thick kelp. Fish over low water into the gullies and holes with a generous fresh crab bait.

Alternatively, try from January to early March when there is a good south-easterly blowing. This can give bags of cod, with a chance of a double. Sport can be equally good in daylight as night.

Distance isn't important unless there is weed around, in which case it may be wise to move. It does not tend to fish well in big exposed seas, mainly those from the north.

Best marks are Schofield rocks, located 100 yards to the left of the path down, and the stone beach near the waterfall.

SPECIES
This is typically a cod venue, but you can get wrasse to 4lb in summer. Occasional coalfish and rockling are caught.

BEST BAITS
In summer it is fresh crabs only. In winter, especially when the weather is hard, cocktail baits with crabs, worms and mussels are very hard to beat.

TACKLE
A good 13ft rock rod for the heavy kelp, matched with a 7000 or 9000-size reel loaded with 30lb line are the basic requirements. Plain leads of 5oz-6oz, attached to a 60lb shockleader, are the mainstay, with a rotten-bottom rig. Use single forged hooks, mainly size 5-6/0, to be able to handle good fish and present a large bait.

GETTING THERE
Located about five miles north of Scarborough, follow the A171 to Cloughton, then take the turning north for Ravenscar and then the right-hand turn for the Hayburn Wyke hotel. Use the car park here, but park away from the hotel to give customers access. Follow the path through the wood to the beach; it's a five-minute walk.

TACKLE SHOP
● **Castle Foot Tackle, 1 Quay St, Scarborough, Tel: 01723 370390.**

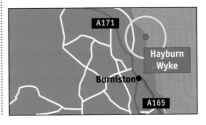

■ *This all-year-round venue is one of the most consistent marks in the country for producing cod. Most of the fishing is done over low water spring tides on the north side of the brigg, when anglers are able to edge along exposed ledges to exploit the vast array of holes and gullies exposed at low tide.*

Best times to fish are when conditions are flat calm. Any sort of a sea can produce dangerous swells that suddenly rise up from the deep water. The hot spot is the brigg end; in summer anglers pack onto this point to plunder the cod that lay tucked under the ledges in the strong tide.

Similar conditions are best suited to low water during darkness in winter. A good south-easterly sea is favoured for the brigg in winter. Fishing in darkness into the south side in the Crab Hole can give excellent bags of codling.

SPECIES
Although cod are this mark's only target in winter, summer fishing can produce coalfish, pollack, wrasse, mackerel, occasional ling and odd conger. Fishing the bay side onto the sand can give flounder, dab, plaice and occasional school bass.

BEST BAITS
In summer the top bait for most species is a fresh peeler crab. However, spinners and small jigs will take mackerel, coalfish, pollack and cod. Worms are the top bait in winter for codling and white rag can be deadly.

TACKLE
The heavy ground is best tackled with a 13ft rock rod, 7000-size multiplier eel with 30lb line and a shockleader. Use a 5oz-6oz plain lead with rotten bottom rigs and size 4/0-5/0 hooks.

However, the back of the brigg and bay side are cleaner ground and can be fished with 6500-size reels loaded with 20lb line and a shockleader. Even lighter specialist gear can be used if you are seeking flatfish or spinning.

GETTING THERE
Filey Brigg is located six miles south of Scarborough along the A165. Follow the signs to Filey, then take the A1039 and then a left turn after the roundabout for the North Country Caravan Park.

Follow the road to the top corner of the site and park. There is an obvious route along the cliff top down onto the brigg; it is possible to see the fishing marks as you are walking along.

TACKLE SHOPS
● *Castle Foot Tackle, 1 Quay St, Scarborough, Tel: 01723 370390.*
● *Scarborough Angling Centre, 7 Market Way, Scarborough, Tel: 01723 381111.*

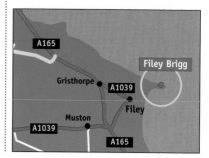

TUNSTALL
Yorkshire

■ *Cod and thornback ray are the two main target species on this part of the Holderness Coast, but this sand and shingle mark can require distance casting due to the shallow water.*

SPECIES
Large numbers of cod and whiting are caught in winter. Summer sees thornback ray, school bass, flounder and eel.

BEST BAITS
Lugworms or squid for cod and whiting; a big ball of lug is favourite. Thornback ray and bass prefer peeler crabs or sandeels. Flounder and eel take fresh peeler crabs.

TACKLE
A standard beach outfit will be more than enough to cope. There are no major snags, so mainline can be 12lb and breakout weights can be between 4oz to 6oz. Use size 3/0 to 5/0 hooks on a running trace for the cod and thornback ray.

GETTING THERE
Tunstall is about six miles south of Aldbrough on the B1242. Once you reach the village, head towards the holiday park find a parking space on the grass verge opposite. A slipway leads to the beach, which is a short walk to the south.

TACKLE SHOP
● *East Coast Tackle, 1b Willow Dr, Hornsea, Tel: 01964 535064.*

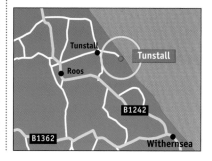

41

■ *Anderby Creek has a reputation for producing fish, yet sometimes when you think conditions are right you won't get a bite.*

The creek is situated between Skegness and Mablethorpe. It is not known as a hard tide beach, but can produce odd codling in winter, while summer sessions give various small species.

This is a mark fished at close range by mostly summer and winter visitors, yet it could produce more fish at distance in the deeper water. Fish after dark at close range.

Big tides and rough sea conditions fished over low water produce the best angling. Fishing over high water is hard work due to high sandbanks and no tidal run.

SPECIES
Codling, sole and flounder.

BEST BAITS
Lugworms can be dug here at low water and are best for codling. A crab bait gives you the edge when fished with lugworms. Small ragworm in bunches, white or harbour rag produce sole and flounder after dark. Use small hooks carrying ragworms or crabs for best results in summer

TACKLE
Standard gear is a 13ft beach rod for off-ground work, while pendulum style casting rods are better for distance work. Most rigs work well here, but a favourite to use is a Pennell with a long snood. Use size 2-2/0 hooks, depending on the fish being sought. The best summer rigs to use are usually Wishbones or three-hooks (size 2) unclipped.

GETTING THERE
Take the B1449 from Alford across the A52 past Huttoft on to Anderby Creek. From Boston, you should stay on the A52 and head for the Chapel signs onto the small coast road and on to the creek. Look out for small beach huts and chalets.

TACKLE SHOP
● *Vanguard Fishing Tackle, Midland Buildings, Skegness Rd, Ingoldmells, Tel: 01754 874950.*

■ *Situated just north of Skegness, this mark is rated as one of the best codling venues on the Lincolnshire coast. March to May produces a spring run of codling.*

The first codling show at the end of September, if the wind is on the north-east quarter. October and November produces fast sport for codling, while December and January slows down.

It is best over high water to get the benefit of the deep water. Fish three hours up to high water and two hours down in winter. Fish tides up to 6.8 metres in rough north-east winds. This beach can be very busy in the summer, so do take extra care while casting.

SPECIES
Summer fishing brings flounder, sole, bass and eel. Codling to 4lb 8oz, with mixed bags of whiting, bass, flounder and dab in winter.

BEST BAITS
Lugworms and peeler crabs. Match anglers use white ragworms for tipping off their baits. Lug tipped with fresh mackerel produces whiting.

TACKLE
A beachcaster with standard multiplier or fixed-spool reel is ideal. Summer rigs are mainly two-up, one-down rigs with size 2 hooks. Use a Pennell rig with size 1 to 1/0 hooks in winter. The snood should be 2ft-3ft long and clipped down.

GETTING THERE
Follow the A52 from Boston to Skegness, going past Butlin's and follow the signs for Fantasy Island. This venue is east of the Fantasy Island leisure complex.

From Alford, take the B1449 to the A52 through Mumby and Hogsthorpe. This goes straight through to Ingoldmells.

TACKLE SHOP
● *Vanguard Fishing Tackle, Midland Buildings, Skegness Rd, Ingoldmells, Tel: 01754 874950.*

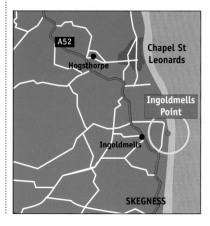

■ *This is an outlet to the sea which is generally fished in summer. It has been claimed that the right tackle could catch tope at the low water deeps, but not many try it..*

It's wise to fish the haven away from the boats and at low water. There is no room to fish when big tides up to seven metres sweep the banks and it can be dangerous. The best time to fish is over high water on small tides.

SPECIES
Summer species are eel, flounder, sole and bass. It is not fished much in winter because other venues offer better fishing.

BEST BAITS
Bait choice is lugworms, harbour rag and crabs. Eel section would be the best bait for a chance of a tope.

TACKLE
Simple tackle can be used because power casting is not involved. Use three-hook paternosters with size 2-4 hooks with up to 6oz of lead weight, depending on the tide run.

Use either a fixed-spool or multiplier reel because lobbing the weight carefully into position is the way to place your bait. Rods can be light sea gear or carp rods.

GETTING THERE
Saltfleet Haven is near Mablethorpe. Take the B1200 from the Louth area and turn on to the A1031 and you are nearly there. Turn right and drive down the side of the Haven. The ground gets soft on the track, so you may have to walk to some fishing spots.

TACKLE SHOP
● *Mablethorpe Angling, 2a-2b Tennison Rd, Mablethorpe, Tel: 01507 478444.*

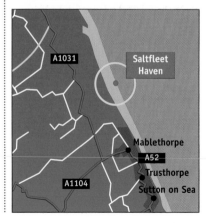

44

■ *This is a busy resort and the beach can get crowded in summer. The beaches around this part of Lincolnshire suffer from lack of depth from time to time at high water.*

They never look like hot spots, but don't rule out catching fish because these beaches can take you by surprise.

SPECIES

Summer anglers fish at low water for flounder, eel and bass. The winter can give codling and whiting over high water. Best winter baits are yellowtail lug tipped with squid or razorfish.

BEST BAITS

Most people use lugworms, but you need peeler crabs and ragworms. Smelly, wrapped lug will take dab.

TACKLE

Light tackle will do the job in summer. Use 12-15lb line with a sufficient shockleader for the lead weight being used. Rigs will be two or three-hook flappers carrying size 2 hooks for flounder, eel, sole and school bass. Bigger hooks are needed for larger bass.

Winter tackle should be heavier to cope with blasting baits out at distance because you need to reach the tide to produce fish. Use 15lb line and a 50-60lb shockleader. Use one or two-hook

clipped rigs with hooks up to size 1/0 big enough. Try fishing from the deepest area to gain more depth. This is a good mark for dab at distance over slack water. You may need up to 6oz of lead in rough conditions.

GETTING THERE

Take the A52 coast road from the Huttoft area past the Sandilands golf course. You will notice beach chalets on top of the sea wall. From Louth, take the A157 on to the A1104 through Mablethorpe and Trusthorpe.

The car park is at the end of the golf course. Walk over the top for easy access.

TACKLE SHOP
● *Vanguard Tackle, 2 Midland Buildings, Ingoldmells, Tel: 01754 874950.*

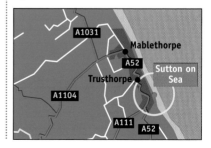

■ *Wolla Bank is one of a string of shallow beaches along the Lincolnshire coast and situated near the Wash.*

Its features can vary from each set of tides from deep to shallow, with gullies at different distances for the beach, as well as clay and underwater forests.

The best tides here are over six metres, but if you are plagued with weed it normally drops off two hours before high water. Best times to fish are over low water or three hours either side of high water.

SPECIES
Fishing is for codling, whiting, bass dab, odd rockling and bullhead.

BEST BAITS
Lugworms and ragworms, with crabs to catch the big flounder and eel. Winter baits are lugworms, razorfish, white rag and squid.

TACKLE
Lightweight tackle is used mostly in summer, with 15lb line and a 60lb shockleader and a 5oz or 6oz lead weight. Heavier tackle is needed to combat the weed and strong tides in winter.

Summer rigs are often three-hooks flapping, while in winter switch to a Pennell or Bomber.

Use size 1 and 2 hooks. Most local match anglers are big casters, but never rule out fishing at 30 yards, if it is slow further out.

GETTING THERE
Take the A52 to Skegness, then go on to Ingoldmells and Chapel St Leonards. Go through Chapel and pass Chapel Point on the coast road, which takes you as far as Mablethorpe.

Other marks are accessible on this road, but Wolla Bank is on the right after Moggs Eye. Beware of parking your vehicle along here at night because there is no street lighting. Park as close to where you are fishing and watch your car.

TACKLE SHOP
● *Vanguard Tackle, 2 Midland Buildings, Ingoldmells, Tel: 01754 874950.*

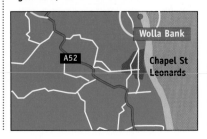

■ This resort mark is fished mainly by holiday makers, who can expect excellent sport in summer.

April to October sees the best of the summer fishing, with the main run of codling in October and November. Best sport on these flat beaches is two hours before high water.

SPECIES
Flounder, eel, sole and bass in summer, with dab and whiting in winter.

BEST BAITS
Lugworms are one of the top all-round. Peeler crabs work when available. Try either king rag or whites for a few sole behind the surf at night in August and September. A large crab or black lug bait fished close in may get a big bass.

TACKLE
Use light tackle because most of the fishing is at close range. A carp or bass rod coupled with a small multiplier or fixed-spool reel, loaded with 15lb line, is ideal. Two or three-hook paternoster rigs and grip leads to 5oz are used.

GETTING THERE
Take the A157 from Lough, then the A1104 to Mablethorpe. Alternatively, follow the main A52 coast road from Skegness through Sutton-on-Sea.

TACKLE SHOPS
● **Humberside Angling Centre, 63-67 Pasture St, Grimsby, Tel: 01472 268988. One of the biggest shops in the country, stocks all major products. Frozen bait always available. Fresh bait available to order. Lugworms imported from Ireland. Fast, friendly, 100% customer service. Two minutes off A180, open seven days a week, Mon-Thurs 8.30am-5.30pm, Fri-Sat 8.30am-6pm, Sunday 8.30am-noon.**
● **Chapman's Sea & Game, 21-29 Beechway, Ashby, Scunthorpe, Tel: 01724 270096.**
● **Cleethorpes Angling Centre, 291 Brereton Avenue, Cleethorpes, Tel: 01472 602002.**

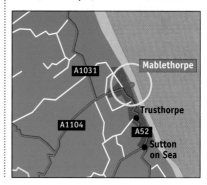

■ *South Eccles is a very consistent snag-free beach of groynes, sand and shingle, but heavy marl at North Eccles means tackle losses can be quite high.*

There are holes within easy casting range from the top of the tide. These can be found by walking the beach at low water. Distance tactics off the bank will reap rewards on the last two hours of the ebb.

SPECIES

Bass, cod, flounder, dab, eel, sole, dogfish, rockling, smoothhound and odd ray.

BEST BAITS

Peeler crabs in summer. A combination of crab and squid is excellent for specimen bass. Lugworms for winter species.

TACKLE

A simple one-up, one-down trace with a 150g-170g lead will cater for all species. Hook lengths should be 20 inches of 20-25lb mono. A reasonable compromise for hooks is a size 1/0 Pennell rig. Use 20-25lb mainline when you fish at North Eccles.

GETTING THERE

Take the A1151 from Norwich signposted to Wroxham and Stalham. At Stalham, take the B1151 signposted to Ingham and then the B1159 to Eccles.

TACKLE SHOP

● *Anglers Armoury, 15 Mundesley Rd, North Walsham, Tel: 01692 403369.*

CAISTER-ON-SEA
Norfolk

■ Caister is just north of the holiday resort of Great Yarmouth and is much quieter than its neighbour. However, the beaches do get busy during peak holiday times.

Tackle losses can be high, especially after a good blow when the beaches can become quite snaggy. The beaches are made up of sand with small patches of shingle. They can shelve off quite steeply, so there can be deep water within easy casting range.

The last three hours of the ebb tide and over low water are the best times.

SPECIES
Cod and whiting in winter. Spring, summer and autumn gives bass, flounder, silver eel, sole and whiting. Spring codling possible.

BEST BAITS
Lugworms, ragworms, fish strip and squid will all catch cod and whiting. Summer baits include peeler crabs, rag and squid.

TACKLE
Be prepared to use at least 6oz of lead on the larger tides, due to the strong currents and possibly weed on an ebbing tide. A standard flowing trace will take cod and bass. A three-hook bomber rig produces catches of flounder, dab and sole.

GETTING THERE
Access on to the beach is clearly signposted off the main A149 road. There is ample car parking available here.

TACKLE SHOP
● *Tackle 'n' Tide, 126 King St, Great Yarmouth, Tel: 01493 852221.*

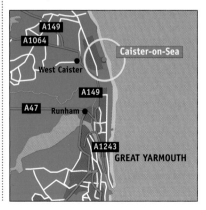

49

■ *The River Great Ouse is a mark with amazing potential. It is a place to go if you enjoy catching lots of fish, yet it is under-fished.*

Fly-fishing for bass and mullet was very popular in the late 1950s and bass to 8lb frequently reached the scales, but this method of fishing is virtually untried here now.

Due to the size, it would take many years to fully appreciate the diversity of fishing the Great Ouse has to offer.

SPECIES
Bass from April. Mullet from the end of May until September, along with large catches of eel and flounder. Sole often venture upriver, while cod show in the lower reaches around November and in April.

BEST BAITS
Use peeler crabs for most species. Ragworms are a good substitute. Bread-tipped harbour rag is top for mullet.

TACKLE
Standard beach gear will cover all requirements, but light tackle can be very exciting. Try the one up, one-down with hook lengths approximately 30 inches long, or float fishing and spinning.

GETTING THERE
King's Lynn is reached on the A47 or A17. You can fish the river in the town or on the outskirts.

TACKLE SHOPS
● *Anglers Corner, 55 London Rd, King's Lynn, Tel: 01553 775852.*
● *Tackle Box, 38 Tower St, King's Lynn, Tel: 01553 761293.*

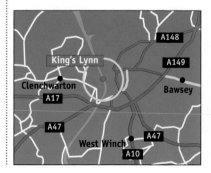

■ *The water here is fairly deep and a short to medium cast will put you in a reasonable depth. Although the beach is made up of sand with just the odd patch of small stone, it can be a little snaggy at times.*

The best state of tide is the whole of the ebb tide and over low water. A walk across the sand to the beach in front of the toilet block can be productive for cod and whiting during the winter.

SPECIES
Spring sees good numbers of dab, flounder and cod caught, while the summer months bring eel, bass, flounder and dab. Cod, dab, flounder and whiting can be caught at this mark through autumn and winter.

BEST BAITS
Crabs and squid cocktails work well for a bass and eel during summer. Lugworms, ragworms and fish strip are the main favourites for the cod, whiting and flatfish.

TACKLE
A simply beach outfit is all that is needed to fish here because distance casting is unnecessary. Great Yarmouth's North Beach has a strong current, especially on the larger tides,

so you will need to use breakout leads of at least 6oz to hold bottom.

GETTING THERE
Follow the A149 coast road to Great Yarmouth. Once there, access to the beach is signposted. There is ample car parking, but it can get very busy in summer.

TACKLE SHOP
● *Tackle 'n' Tide, 126 King St, Great Yarmouth, Tel: 01493 852221.*

51

■ The beach is mainly sand with the odd patch of shingle and small stone. Gullies give way to sandbanks that can be uncovered and which dry out on large, low tides.

The water here is quiet and shallow and is virtually unfishable during rough seas. Most productive time is three hours before high tide and two hours down. Sometimes weed can be a problem. On a really big tide, low water can produce good catches of dab and flounder, which can be caught all year. Aim to fish the gullies in between the sandbanks and shore. These can be anywhere between 50 yards and 150 yards from the high tide mark.

SPECIES
Besides the dab and flounder, you'll get the cod in winter and spring, eel with the odd bass and sole in summer, and whiting during the autumn.

BEST BAITS
Ragworms, lugworms and fish strip are best for the flatfish, whiting and cod. Use crabs and squid for bass and eel.

TACKLE
This is mainly a medium to long range casting beach, so use standard beach gear and 15lb mainline. Two or three hook paternoster rigs are favoured. Clipped-down versions will help casting distance. Pennell rigs can be used for bigger baits.

GETTING THERE
Mundesley is east of Cromer along the B1159 coast road. Access to the beaches is signposted in and around the village. The main car park is on the sea front, opposite the slope leading onto the beach. This is a pay and display car park in summer.

TACKLE SHOP
● *Marine Sports, 21 New St, Cromer, Tel: 01263 513676.*

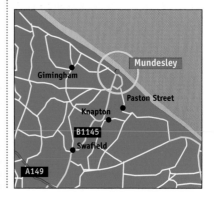

■ There are eight reefs here, four at 250 metres long and four at 50 metres, designed to protect the exposed beaches.

Deep lagoons have been created between the reefs and should be fished three hours up and two hours over the top. The reefs are dangerous, so night fishing at Sea Palling is not recommended and should be avoided.

SPECIES
Cod, bass, whiting, sole, eel, dogfish, smoothhound, coalfish and plaice are the mainstay. Whiting and cod show from late October through to January. There should be a spring run of codling during the second set of big tides in

March and could still show as late as May.

Spring and summer offer the best chances of bass, dab and flounder during daylight, with smoothhound, sole, dogfish and eel at night.

BEST BAITS
As soon as the first peeler crabs start to show, they become the prime bait. Whole squid is an option for a cod or bass on a spare rod, but lug comes into their own after the first autumn frosts. Sandeels can be effective when fished under a float for bass.

TACKLE
Standard beach gear or a spinning rod can be used here. Reefs one and two are accessible during the last three hours of the ebb tide and can be good for spinning or legering or even dinghy fishing.

GETTING THERE
Take the A1151 from Norwich, to Wroxham and Stalham. Follow the B1151 from Stalham. It changes to the B1159 to take you to Sea Palling.

TACKLE SHOPS
● *Country Pursuits, 49 Market Place, North Walsham, Tel: 01692 403162.*
● *Marine Sports, 21 New St, Cromer, Tel: 01263 513676.*

53

■ *The town beach is where the commercial fishermen keep their boats. The beach requires careful selection before starting to fish, particularly at night because the boats tend to leave early in the morning.*

The water here is still fairly deep and the species vary from cod, whiting and bass to dab, flounder

and sole. There are frequently small dogfish and the occasional tope during the summer.

SPECIES
Codling, whiting, bass, dogfish, dab, flounder and sole.

BEST BAITS
Lugworms, mackerel, squid and razorfish, with ragworms doing well, especially in summer.

TACKLE
Use standard beach tackle, with a two-hook paternoster rig or the sliding leger with a two-hook Pennell.

GETTING THERE
Aldeburgh is clearly signposted from the A12 towards Lowestoft.

TACKLE SHOP
● *Tackle Up, Walton High Street, Felixstowe, Tel: 01394 274600.*

■ *Landguard is a shingle beach giving way to clean sand and is renowned for its good bass and sole sport.*

A sandbank runs parallel to the beach about 150 yards out and comes closer about 70 yards nearer to the river mouth. Landguard beach is mainly a spring, summer and autumn venue. Late evening tides fished into the night will bring best fishing. Fish two hours up to high tide and two hours down.

SPECIES
Bass, sole, dab, eel and flounder.

BEST BAITS
King ragworms and lugworms both work well for sole, while ragworms, peeler crabs or a whole squid can tempt bass. Try experimenting with different cocktails for the flounder and eel. Try a whole squid on 5ft flowing trace cast 20 yards for the best chance of a bass.

TACKLE
Standard beach gear is required, but try using a bass or carp rod and lighter line. Three-hook flapping rigs take sole, with a long, single-hook flowing top trace for bass.
The most prolific species tend to hug the

shoreline, so a cast of between 20-60 yards puts you among the bass and sole.

GETTING THERE
Take the A14 off the A12 towards Felixstowe and follow the signs for Felixstowe docks and then for the seafront. Follow the signs to Landguard Fort and the beach is clearly visible.

TACKLE SHOP
● *Tackle Up, 288 High St, Walton, Felixstowe, Tel: 01394 274600.*

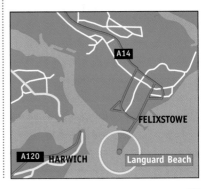

LOWESTOFT SOUTH PIER
Suffolk

■ *This 300-yard long solid pier borders the entrance to the harbour and fishing port and is popular with anglers of all ages. It provides a good mix of fishing on the outside, plus excellent sport inside.*

SPECIES
Eel, dogfish, flounder and bass are the fish that form the bulk of summer catches. October to January produces cod, whiting, and dab. Spring codling can arrive in March or April. Sole show from July to September.

BEST BAITS
Use lugworms in winter, peeler crabs in spring and summer for cod and bass. Lug or rag on small hooks take dab and sole. Mullet, flounder and bass are taken on the inside of the pier. Whiting prefer lug and mackerel combinations.

TACKLE
Light tackle is all you need because distance casting is not required. A rod capable of casting a 3oz-4oz lead is suitable. A two-hook rig will cover most eventualities at this mark. Mullet need freshwater float tackle and groundbaiting with mashed bread.

A Pennell rig and grip lead is favoured in winter for cod. Long snoods attached near the lead work well for all species. Take a drop-net.

GETTING THERE
Take the A12, which goes directly to Lowestoft, then follow the signs leading to the harbour. There is parking nearby.

TACKLE SHOP
● *Ding-Its Tackle Den, London Rd, Pakefield Lowestoft, Tel: 01502 519483.*

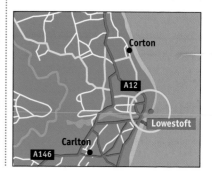

going up from the standard 5oz breakaway leads to 6oz in the strongest tides.

The Pennell rig with size 2/0 hooks will cover almost all eventualities. For Dover sole at the narrows in summer, switch to a two-hook paternoster size 2 with or without booms.

It is wise to take a good shelter, warm clothing and plenty of food and drink.

BEST BAITS
Peeler crabs are by far the best all-round bait, although sole normally take only ragworms or lugworms. A small ragworm often produces a pouting, which makes an excellent livebait for bass, especially at the Narrows at dawn.

Lug are the killer bait for winter cod. Blow lug are the local version, but black lug or yellowtails work. Squid cocktailed with lug or on its own can also be excellent.

GETTING THERE
From the main A12, between Woodbridge and Saxmundham, take the A1094 which is signposted Aldeburgh. Turn right at the Snape crossroads onto the B1069, then immediately after passing Snape Maltings take the left turn onto the by-road signposted Orford. Drive through Sudbourne and onto Orford. The quay is at the end of the road and a large car park is within walking distance.

TACKLE SHOP
● *Tackle Up, Walton High Street, Felixstowe, Tel: 01394 274600.*

■ *Orford is one of the best cod beaches in the country. A very steep shingle bank falls straight into water about 15 feet deep, creating excellent conditions for catching cod and this shingle forms the southern end of a spit which runs from Aldeburgh in the north almost ten miles away.*
The whole area is now managed by The National Trust, who control access points and the pathways over the spit to the seaward side. In fact the only way to get across to the island is by ferry from the town of Orford.
Normally the ferry will leave Orford Quay at 8am and return at 4pm. Alternatively, going out at 4pm and coming back the following morning at 8am satisfies those anglers who do not need to sleep and prefer to fish all night. You should book this in advance – speak to the local tackle shop for a contact point.

SPECIES
Cod are the winter target, but codling can show in spring as well. Summer fishing is good for bass, sole, dogfish, porting and eel. There are occasional bonus catches of spurdog, smoothhound and thornback ray.

TACKLE
The strong tide run means that long distance casting is not required. A good quality, middle to top-of-the-range, 12ft beachcaster works well. Line is normally 15lb or 18lb breaking strain and a 60lb shockleader is a must. This also allows for

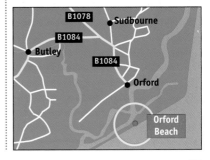

■ *The warm water outlets of power stations on this beach attract a wide range of species.*

Fish are close in, but anglers who can cast 100 yards will find better catches outside the sandbar, which runs around the bay.

SPECIES
Main summer target is bass and, while the fish are mainly small schoolies around the outlets, much better specimens rove along the beach from Minsmere sluice north and around the bay towards Thorpeness Point.

Night fishing in summer yields catches of sole

to 2lb. The occasional stingray has been taken in recent years. Autumn sees the arrival of huge shoals of whiting, especially on evening tides. The run of cod during November and December will again favour the long distance caster.

BEST BAITS
King ragworms are best in summer, although the bigger bass like whole squid, mackerel fillet, peeler crabs or live pouting. Best winter bait is lug, which is tipped with mackerel for the whiting or squid for cod. Frozen sandeels should be tried for a change.

TACKLE
This is a bottom-fishing venue, which needs 5oz leads and a powerful rod. Lighter tackle comes into its own for the bass and sole in summer.

GETTING THERE
From the A12 between Farnham and Yoxford, take the B1119 to Leiston and then drive on to the sea at Sizewell.

TACKLE SHOP
● *Saxmundham Angling Centre, Market Place, Saxmundham, Tel: 01728 603443.*

■ *Thorpeness Point attracts a good variety of species throughout the year. The strong tide run across the point creates a series of banks and gullies within casting range. The back eddy on the north side of the point creates deep water and plenty of food.*

SPECIES

Bass to 8lb show, although some specimens over 10lb have been taken. Dover sole appear on the north side during the summer. From the end of August, whiting arrive on the right tides and they start to thin out in October. This is the time codling show up and they have been caught south of Thorpeness Point before any other mark on the Suffolk coast.

With flounder, pouting and rockling always around, this is a mark for all seasons.

BEST BAIT

King ragworms, frozen sandeel or squid for bass. King rag also take sole, which also like lug and rag cocktails. Whiting eat virtually anything, but codling like peeler crabs in early autumn, but switch for lug or squid as the water cools.

TACKLE

Standard tackle is a beachcaster capable of handling a 5oz breakout lead. You will need a tripod. A running leger rig carrying a Pennell set up with size 4/0 hooks is best for bass. Use a single 4/0 Viking to carry a frozen sandeel.

King rag on size 2 Aberdeens on a paternoster rig are favoured for sole.

GETTING THERE

Follow the A12 between Southwold and Ipswich, then take the A1094 towards Aldeburgh and the B1353 direct to Thorpeness. Access requires a half-mile walk under the cliffs, which may deter some anglers. Those with strong legs can find space and solitude.

TACKLE SHOP

● *Saxmundham Angling Centre, Market Place, Saxmundham, Tel: 01728 603443.*

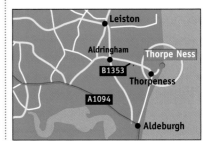

CLIFF ROAD
Holland-on-Sea, Essex

■ *This is a popular summer and winter venue for anglers of all abilities.*

The best fishing is over the top of the tide after dark for the winter species. Late in the evening or early in the morning is the top period for bass, while daylight fishing is always worth a try.

SPECIES
Flounder, bass, codling and whiting.

BEST BAITS
Lugworms in winter, with peeler crabs and ragworms in summer.

TACKLE
You will need about 6oz of grip lead to hold bottom during the favoured spring tides. Summer fishing for eel requires size 2 hooks. Bass are caught to float tactics or artificial eels cast out a few yards.

GETTING THERE
Take the A133 into Clacton and follow the signs to the sea front. Turn left towards Holland-on-Sea and pass the Kingscliff Hotel. A quarter of a mile further on you will see a large grass sitting area, where steps go down on to the beach.

TACKLE SHOP
● *Brian Dean Tackle, 43 Pallister Rd, Clacton, Tel: 01255 425992.*

DOVERCOURT BEACH
Essex

■ *This is a shallow beach with groynes along its entire two mile length. The extreme east end is bordered by the stone pier and the west end consists of a large breakwater, known as the Smack.*

Either end of the beach offers the best sport, rather than the middle.

Best stage of the tide for most species is from high water down. April gives good bags of eel during the first three hours of the flood.

SPECIES
School bass and eel from May onwards. June to

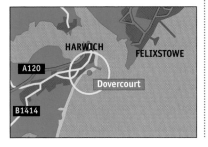

September can give occasional sole. Late September onwards offers mainly codling and whiting. There are a few flounder caught all year.

BEST BAITS
A fresh peeler crab is the main spring bait, but ragworms work as the weather gets warmer. Lug tipped with fish catch in autumn and winter.

TACKLE
Standard beachcasting gear with a 5oz grip lead is needed. A one-up, one-down rig with size 2 hooks catches most species. On the bigger tides a bomber or see-saw wishbone rig will fish well at distance.

GETTING THERE
Dovercourt is on a peninsula. Follow the A120 to Dovercourt and then pick up signs for the sea front. There is ample parking.

TACKLE SHOP
● *Meta-Lite Tackle, 15 Newgate St, Walton-on-the-Naze, Tel: 01255 675680.*

61

■ *Frinton wall runs between Holland-on-Sea and Frinton and is an area for those anglers who can cast about 100 yards with bait.*

This is one of the most popular areas along this part of the Essex coast because of the good numbers of large cod caught each year.

One of the problems is landing a fish, so familiarise yourself with the best spots. It's too late when you have a cod on the end. A dull day or night fishing on spring tides is best.

SPECIES
Expect to catch whiting and cod in winter, with occasional bass.

BEST BAITS
Use large baits made from lugworms, but try peeler crabs early in the season.

TACKLE
Normal beach tackle capable of casting a 6oz lead weight is ideal. It is best to use a single bait and then cast as far as you can.

GETTING THERE
It is best to go on to the wall from the Frinton side. Take the B1033 into Frinton and follow the main road down to the sea front. At the end of the road, turn right and go as far as you can. Park at the end and walk along the wall. Fish anywhere past the beach huts, but the golf course area is best.

TACKLE SHOP
● *Meta-Lite Tackle, 15 Newgate St, Walton-on-the-Naze, Tel: 01255 675680.*

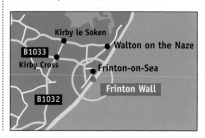

■ The Halfpenny Pier provides easy access to deep water and fast tides at the mouth of the rivers Stour and Orwell.

This north-facing wooden structure fishes well throughout the year. Despite the quality of its fishing, it is generally under-fished. The sheltered location means it is always fishable.

SPECIES
Flounder, dab and small whiting early in the year. April sees the arrival of eel. There is also a run of thornback ray. Night fishing gives bass towards the end of summer. A flooding tide in autumn is best for sole. Shortly after this, hordes of whiting invade the area, then codling.

BEST BAITS
Ragworms and crabs in the summer. Black artificial eels are best for the bass at night. Lugworms, sandeels and squid heads for the winter fish.

TACKLE
Fish under the pier with strong tackle; fish up to 5lb feature regularly and every year sees a handful of fish up to double figures. Multi-hook rigs account for the majority of fish. Distance tactics produce the thornback ray and codling.

GETTING THERE
Follow the A12 northbound, then turn off and take the A120 towards Harwich. Look for the signs for Navy yard wharf; the pier is located next to this. There is ample free parking on either side of the mark.

TACKLE SHOPS
● *Meta-Lite Tackle, 15 Newgate St, Walton-on-the-Naze, Tel: 01255 675680.*

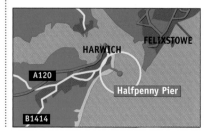

■ The Crouch is a narrow river extending from Battlesbridge to Wallasea Island and Foulness Island on the southern side and Burnham on the north side.

Notable marks are Wallasea Island, Black Point at Canewdon, South Fambridge and Hullbridge on the south side, or Althorne and Hollywell Point beyond Burnham on the north side.

Winter sport is towards the outer estuary, with Hollywell and Wallasea favoured. Access is limited and can mean a fair walk.

A mark called The Hole, about half a mile from Essex Marina at Wallasea, offers fishing along a stretch of sea wall, which can be easily reached. It was at Essex Marina in 2002 that a massive 11lb mullet was caught by a junior angler. The river can also be fished from its north bank at Burnham-on-Crouch.

Low water up and one hour down at night is usually best, but calm summer evenings are good.

SPECIES
Some of the best summer fishing is from the small creeks, where bass can be caught. There is excellent sport for eel, flounder, mullet and dab. Whiting and some codling in winter.

BEST BAITS
Use peeler crabs and ragworms in summer and lugworms in winter.

TACKLE
A beachcaster and reel is fine, but you can have more fun with school bass on a light spinning outfit. Rigs should incorporate a size 1/0 to 3/0 Aberdeen hook and use a 4oz-6oz breakout weight. Don't cast too far.

GETTING THERE
From the A127, take the B1013 towards Rochford, then turn right towards Great Stambridge. Follow this road to its end and turn right towards Paglesham. A left turn goes to Canewdon and then right towards Essex Marina.

TACKLE SHOP
● Jetty Anglers, 47 Eastern Esplanade, Southend Tel: 01702 611826.

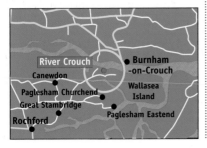

■ *This is the longest pleasure pier in the world and offers great potential for sea anglers.*
The pier head extension faces deep water and the favourite marks are the east and west points. The south face is snaggy.

Approaching the south station, there is no fishing on that part of the pier's west side denoted by yellow lines. On the east side, anglers must avoid the RNLI launching area and a separate slipway.

The stem of the pier dries at low water, so fishing is restricted to three hours either side of high water. Sport further towards the shore usually results in only flounder.

At the time of going to press, daytime admission was £3.20 (£2 concessions) April to September inclusive; £2.60 (£1.80) October to March. These charges include the return fare on the pier train. The annual day and night pass costs £81.50, night pass alone is £38.50, day-only pass is £43 (£21 juniors).

SPECIES
Garfish, mackerel, school bass, flounder, mullet, eel and odd plaice in summer. Whiting, pouting, dab and cod in winter.

BEST BAITS
Best baits are lugworms in winter, peeler crabs in summer. Mackerel strip fished in mid-water to the surface is good for mackerel and garfish. Use peeler crabs and ragworms as bottom baits for the other species. Lures are effective at times for bass. Small ragworms are favoured for mullet. Small livebaits pick up the better bass in summer and autumn.

TACKLE
Standard beach gear can be used here, although lighter tackle, even an uptide boat rod, can be used in summer if you want to try float fishing or feathering.

Use two or three-hook paternoster rigs or float outfits. Try a single-hook rig or Pennell for bigger baits.

GETTING THERE
Approaching from the M25, Southend is reached on the A127 or A13 towards Basildon. Both roads take you into Southend, where you follow the signs to the seafront. You can't miss the pier.

TACKLE SHOP
● *Jetty Anglers, 47 Eastern Esplanade, Southend Tel: 01702 611826.*

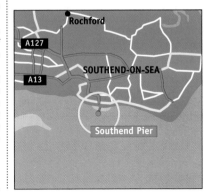

■ *The Admiralty pier stretches half a mile into the sea and includes 500 angling spaces.*

Hot spots include the pier end during an ebb tide and the seaward side of the turret at high water. The end fishes best after high water as the strong tide eases. Casting is hampered by a tall fence, but a 30-yard lob often brings results.

Tickets are £3.50 for Dover SAA members (non-members £5), available at the main entrance or on the pier when busy. The pier is open between 8am and 4pm during winter and all-night fishing over Friday and Saturday nights only.

Dover SAA runs the pier. For club bookings, fixtures, Tel: 01304 204722. Direct line to pier, Tel: 01304 225138.

SPECIES
Large numbers of mackerel are caught on feathers during June and August, while bass, mullet, plaice, pollack, scad, dogfish and pouting are also landed.

BEST BAITS
Yellowtail lugworms, king ragworms, peeler crabs and squid are the best baits, with harbour rag and bread suitable for mullet.

TACKLE
Strong tides experienced during high water means a 6oz lead is essential to hold bottom. During spring tides, an 8oz lead may be too light. A short trace is successful in a strong tide with a mono paternoster ideal at all other times.

GETTING THERE
To reach the pier, follow Snargate Street via the A2 or A20.

TACKLE SHOP
● **Channel Angling, 158-160 Snargate St, Dover, Tel: 01304 203742.**

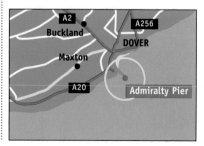

lugworms and fish baits score for winter whiting. Ragworms catch some of the summer species.

TACKLE

Two hooks cast at distance are most likely to produce fish in summer and winter. Short range casting alongside the groyne can produce the odd bass, but distance improves your chances, due to the shallow nature of the area. Wading produces fish at low water.

You will need a breakout lead, although the tide is only medium strength at Beltinge promenade. Despite the shallow water, bass get close to the shoreline here between June and October with an edible peeler or a large ragworm the top bait.

GETTING THERE

From the M2 motorway, take the A299 at Junction 7 towards Herne Bay. Take the roundabout after the Herne Bay town centre. There is parking on the cliff above the shore, followed by a long walk down steps to the shoreline and promenade.

TACKLE SHOPS

● *Bowlers Angling Centre, 2-3 Cinema Parade, Dagenham, Tel: 0208 984 7533.*
● *Mark 2 Angling, 24-26 The High St, Crayford, Tel: 01322 554545.*

■ *The stretch of promenade at Beltinge is best fished over high water or during a rising tide.*

The hot time for eel is during the ebb. Low water fishing requires boots because there is mud close to the groyne ends. A long mussel bank, called the Rand, which is situated at the base of the Beltinge steps, offers a vantage point for low tide bass anglers.

SPECIES

You can catch flounder, eel, bass and odd stingray in spring and summer. Most whiting and some codling in winter.

BEST BAITS

Peeler crabs are best most of the time, although

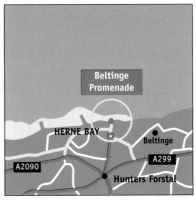

67

DOVER SOUTHERN BREAKWATER
Kent

■ *Dover's breakwater guards the entrance to the harbour and its angling potential is enormous.*

Nicknamed the concrete boat, it can only be reached from the sea and boats set off from Wellington dock pontoon at 8.30am before returning at 3.30pm on Wednesdays, Saturdays and Sundays only (weather permitting – wind under Force 7 on current BBC Shipping Forecast). Night fishing is available through the Dover SAA only. The motor boat company's return fare to the breakwater is £3, Tel: 01304 204722.

Fishing tickets cost £3.50 for Dover SAA members (£5 non-members, including temporary membership). Contact Dover SAA, Tel: 01304 204722. Club bookings etc, Alan Edgington, Tel: 01303 822864.

SPECIES
The variety is huge, but bass, mackerel, mullet and flounder show in summer. Cod and whiting sport dominates in winter.

BEST BAITS
Yellowtail lugworms and peeler crabs are the top winter baits for cod, while king rag and harbour rag are good for pollack and flounder in summer. Fresh mackerel, herring or cuttlefish will catch dogfish, while bread tempts mullet. Feathers catch mackerel in clear water.

TACKLE
Use standard beach tackle, but the very strong tides here at high and low water require weights with nose grip wires.

A favourite rig is a two-up, one-down with longish snoods. Size 1 hooks are good, but size 3/0 should be used for the bigger winter cod and summer bass.

GETTING THERE
Follow the M20 until the A20. Turn right at the third roundabout as you enter Dover. You will be within walking distance of Wellington dock and limited parking is available.

TACKLE SHOP
● *Channel Angling, 158-160 Snargate St, Dover, Tel: 01304 203742.*

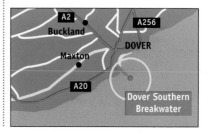

FOLKESTONE PIER
Kent

■ *This is an ideal venue for beginners because it does not feature the strong tides of the others in Kent. Fishing is available throughout its length, but not at the end or on the harbour side. Day and night tickets are available.*

Best results are during the strongest tidal movement and you need to fish two hours either side of high water. Both darkness and coloured water improve results.

The end gets some ebb tide run at low water. Fish the low peg numbers, near the end at low water, and the high numbers at high water. The first bend is the hot spot for flatfish.

Run by Folkestone SAA, tickets are available at the town's tackle shops (see below) for £3.50 (not available at pier). The pier is open 9am to 9pm, and all night at weekends. Ticket details and club bookings, Phil Tanner, Tel: 01303 220763.

SPECIES

Codling, pouting, whiting and dab are possible from autumn through to March. In summer, there are mackerel, pollack, scad, bass, eel, plaice and some small pouting.

BEST BAITS

Lugworms are best. Others include squid in winter, both as a tip bait or whole for larger fish. Peeler crabs, white rag and red rag all catch. Fresh fish is good in January for flatfish.

TACKLE

Use a fixed-grip lead to hold bottom at high water, although the current is only fierce during the spring tides, when a Gemini red head is enough to hold bottom.

Three-hook paternoster rigs are favoured with size 1 hooks to 25lb snoods to catch dab, whiting and pouting, but able to hold the odd cod. Apart from the legering, booms or light tackle fished off the bottom, alongside the wall, account for pollack, bass, mullet and scad, while a large mackerel bait fished down the wall gets some conger.

Snags out from the wall can be a problem, especially during strong spring tides.

GETTING THERE

Folkestone is at the end of the M2. Head for the channel tunnel and once in the town go to the sea front. Drive in, park and walk along the railway platform. A set of steps takes you up to the pier promenade.

Tickets must be purchased before you enter and are available from the tackle shop within 400 yards of the pier entrance.

TACKLE SHOPS
● *Folkestone Angling, 12 Tontine Street, Folkestone, Tel: 01303 253381.*
● *Harbour Tackle, 10 Beach St, Folkestone, Tel: 01303 220763.*

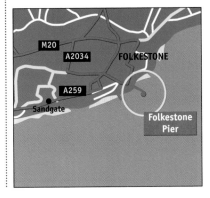

■ Hythe seafront is a good winter mark where you can fish from your car at half of the venue, while the other half requires a short walk to reach the promenade.

Some good catches of flatfish are made in the New Year close to the various groyne ends, although weather distance is an advantage at other times and in calmer weather.

Best results come at the top and just after high tide with westerly storms; coloured water or darkness being most likely to produce fish. Low tide fishes occasionally during or after a south-west gale. Spring tides are best with high water between 9pm and 2am.

SPECIES

Codling, whiting, pouting, dab, flounder, poor cod and rockling in winter. Pouting, sole, eel, bass, dogfish, mackerel, plaice and scad in summer.

BEST BAITS

Black lugworms and common lug. Fresh yellowtails have their day for whiting, pouting and codling, while slightly stale blacks are excellent for dab and sole, and in February the rockling.

Herring or mackerel-tipped worm baits work for whiting, while a small live pouting is an excellent autumn bait for bass.

TACKLE

Two or three-hook paternosters and size 1 long-shank hooks are preferred with a 5oz breakout lead sufficient to hold the strongest tide, which travels west to east over high water. The ebb tide flow is minimal.

GETTING THERE

Hythe is on the A259 between Dymchurch and Folkestone and you get to Marine Parade by turning seawards at the town centre along Twiss Road, Stade Street and St Leonard's Street.

TACKLE SHOP

● *Marsh Tackle, 17 Littlestone Rd, New Romney, Kent, Tel: 01797 366130.*

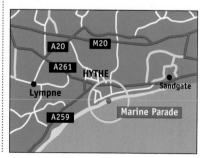

70

■ *The remains of a Roman fort lie at this popular mark. The venue is weedy after a storm with the hour after high water almost impossible to fish on some spring tides.*

Good catches come from the sand at low water, especially from the bank north of the towers.

SPECIES
Eel, bass and flounder are caught in summer and

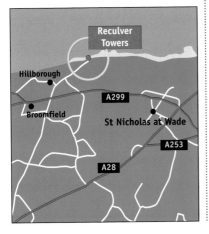

there is a chance of stingray, thornback ray and smoothhound. The venues produces plenty of whiting on calm winter nights and occasional cod to 20lb.

BEST BAITS
Peeler crabs are the only bait worth using in spring and summer, with a half crab fished on size 1 hooks. In winter, black lugworms, crabs, mackerel strip and white rag will catch whiting, flounder, rockling and cod.

TACKLE
Most anglers use two or three hooks fished paternoster style. Although the venue looks rocky, tackle losses are limited.

GETTING THERE
Take the A299 towards Ramsgate. The Reculver turning is signposted after Herne Bay. Turnings to Beltinge and Hillborough lead to Reculver and the car park.

TACKLE SHOPS
● *Bowlers Angling Centre, 2-3 Cinema Parade, Dagenham, Tel: 0208 984 7533.*
● *Mark 2 Angling, 24-26 The High St, Crayford, Tel: 01322 554545.*

■ *Situated quite close to Brighton town centre, this huge construction provides a really superb angling venue.*

The marina comprises east and west arms, and the ground is of mixed nature, ranging from medium rock to clean sand. The cleanest ground and sandiest area is found beyond the bend on the longer eastern arm, where you can fish the inside as well.

At the time of going to press, tickets were £2 per rod all day (eight hours) or £1.50 concessions; available from the Tackle Box. A twilight package is available.

SPECIES
Plenty of garfish, mackerel and some pollack are caught in summer. Mullet are present during settled weather and some huge bass are landed every year. Dogfish, gurnard and pouting are taken from the sandy areas, along with sole at

night. Autumn brings brisk sport with whiting and cod after winter gales.

BEST BAITS
For general fishing, use ragworms, lugworms, peeler crabs and fish strip. Large bass are caught by presenting a live pouting or joey mackerel on a size 6/0 hook lowered down the side.

TACKLE
Standard beach tackle will cope with most situations on the cleaner areas. A fast-retrieve reel with 25lb straight through will keep tackle losses to a minimum. A light rod with a fixed-spool reel is a handy addition in the summer for float fishing or spinning.

GETTING THERE
Take the slip road off the A259, one-and-a-half miles east of the town centre. Fishing tickets for the marina are available from the Tackle Box shop on the Marina.

Obtain a voucher from the Tackle Box to gain 24-hour parking in the multi-storey car park. Toilets are located on the west arm.

TACKLE SHOP
● *The Tackle Box, Brighton Marina, Brighton, Tel: 01273 696477.*

72

■ *This spring and summer mark, known locally at Cliff End, is 300 yards long and found at the western end of the Pett Levels and the beginning of Fairlight Cliffs.*

This is a shallow area and mainly sandy with odd patches of rock, boulders and gullies. Most fish are caught on the low water and first two hours of the flood tide.

SPECIES
Bass and silver eel dominate catches, but expect some good flounder if the sea has some colour. Plenty of codling and whiting can be taken after dark in winter.

BEST BAITS
Black lugworms work well, as do peeler crabs during the April to July period. Both lug and crabs can be collected from the Pett Levels. Razorfish and butterfish can be good for flounder after winter gales.

TACKLE
You need a standard beachcaster with 15lb mainline and 150g breakout lead. Use size 2 and 1 hooks. A rolling lead works well for the flounder.

GETTING THERE
Take the A259 east from Hastings and turn right into Fairlight Road, proceeding to Pett Level (five miles). Turn right 100 yards past the village store, where there is a small car park. From there, it is a 300-yard walk to the beach.

TACKLE SHOP
● *Hastings Angling Centre, 33 The Bourne, Hastings, Tel: 01424 432178.*

■ *The longer west arm protecting the harbour at Hastings provides easy access to a comfortable fishing platform.*

The concrete arm is about 60 yards long, so it is best fished over the high water period from either side. Cast west into the open sea and deep water and a good tide run, or you can cast east into the harbour.

SPECIES

Being productive throughout the year, species include codling, whiting, dab, flounder, bass, plaice, sole, dogfish, smoothhound, eel, mullet, garfish and mackerel.

BEST BAITS

Lugworms are best, but ragworms, squid, fish, shellfish, peeler crabs, harbour rag and bread all work for various species at certain times.

Fish a bunch of harbour rag in the harbour for flounder from December until March. Mullet like a constant supply of mashed bread down the side of the wall.

TACKLE

The ground at this mark is fairly clean, so a normal beachcaster and small multiplier or fixed-spool reel, loaded with 15-18lb line, are ideal. Locals use two rods – one on each side. A lighter estuary-type rod is better for casting inside the harbour.

Use two or three-hook paternoster rigs with hooks from size 4 to size 2/0. Breakout leads up to 190g are required.

GETTING THERE

Go east along Hastings seafront, the A259. Hastings and St Leonards SAA clubhouse is half a mile past the pier on the right. Turn right 100 yards past here into a pay-and-display car park. The harbour arm is behind the lifeboat station.

TACKLE SHOP

● *Steve's Tackle Shop, 38 White Rock, Hastings, Tel: 01424 433404.*

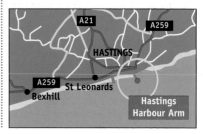

■ *Piddinghoe is an easy-access section of the River Ouse about one-and-a-half miles above Newhaven and three miles from the open sea.*
Most fish at Piddinghoe are taken either during the first two hours of the flood or during the first two hours of the ebb.

SPECIES

Thousands of peeler crabs enter the river from late March, and these creatures attract silver eel, flounder and bass. Bags of eels exceeding 25lb are taken. Large numbers of mullet are present from mid-May during the last two or three hours of the ebb tide.

BEST BAITS

Peeler crabs, bread, ragworms.

TACKLE

Tidal flow can be extremely swift, so you will need breakout leads up to 150g during the fierce early flood and ebb, when weed is being carried through. Reduce your lead size as the tide eases.

A light bass rod or stepped-up carp rod, carrying a small multiplier or fixed-spool with 12lb-15lb mainline, is ideal. You can fish safely with a 25lb shockleader because only a gentle lob is required.

A simple one-up, one-down paternoster rig with long snoods carrying size 2 Kamasan B980 short-shank hooks will get good results. Mullet require a match or Avon-type coarse rod with a fixed-spool reel loaded with 4lb-5lb line. Thick-lips are best sought by float fishing after groundbaiting. Best method for thin-lips is to cast and retrieve a spoon baited with ragworms over high water.

GETTING THERE

Turn north into Lewes Road from the Newhaven ring road (A259). Proceed for a mile and a half and turn right at the Piddinghoe sign. There is ample free parking when you get there.

TACKLE SHOP

● *The Tackle Box, Brighton Marina, Brighton, Tel: 01273 696477.*

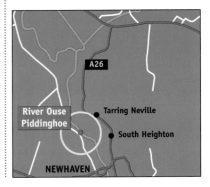

ROTTINGDEAN
Sussex

■ *A very popular bass fishing mark where the beach is conveniently accessible next to a public car park. The beach is mainly rock and primarily a summer bass venue, but produces cod in winter.*

The bass hot spot is next to the pipe in front of the High Street. Fish after dark over high water. A spring tide increases your chances of a good fish.

SPECIES
Bass and cod.

BEST BAITS
Big crab baits. Experiment with mackerel, pouting, squid and cuttlefish in the autumn when specimen fish are taken on large baits.

TACKLE
Use a single size 5/0 or 6/0 hook and a rotten-bottom attachment on your rig. A fast-retrieve reel will reduce tackle loss. Locals use 25lb-28lb line and dispense with a shockleader because long casting is unnecessary.

GETTING THERE
Rottingdean is on the A259 coast road three miles east of Brighton. Park in the public car park behind the White Horse pub. The concrete slope leads to the beach area.

TACKLE SHOP
● *The Tackle Box, Brighton Marina, Brighton, Tel: 01273 696477.*

TIDEMILLS
Newhaven, Sussex

■ *This beach is between Seaford and the eastern arm at Newhaven and is noted for golden grey mullet and flounder.*

Long tides in daylight produce more fish, so start two hours up from low water, but don't expect much from two hours after high water.

SPECIES

Noted for mullet, but other species include cod, whiting, bass, dab, eel, plaice, gurnard, dragonet, garfish and mackerel. Whiting and codling are caught after dark in winter, but Seaford town beach is a better option for these.

BEST BAITS

Mullet take a bunch of harbour ragworms, while flounder like rag, razorfish, butterfish and mussels. Lugworms tipped with a strip of mackerel is best for whiting. A thin strip of mackerel or strip under a float over high tide in summer gets garfish and mackerel.

TACKLE

A carp rod or light bass rod is best for mullet. A small multiplier or fixed-spool reel carrying 12-15lb mainline and a 25lb shockleader is ideal.
A one-up, one-down rig with size 4 or 6 hooks on 12-15lb snoods will attract most bites. Use leads up to 4oz. Optimum casting range is 30-50 yards. Winter flounder can be caught on the

same gear during fine weather, but step up as the weather worsens.

Garfish can be caught by using a flier rig slid down the mainline while bottom fishing for mullet. Bait the float rig with a slither of fish on a size 6 hook and set at three feet deep.

GETTING THERE

Go west from Seaford on the A259 and turn left half-a-mile past the motel, into Mill Drive Lane. Go a further 300 yards, then park in the lay-by on the left. After this, a 600-yard walk is required, by continuing along the lane through the railway crossing.

TACKLE SHOP

● *Newhaven Angler, Fort Rd, Newhaven, Tel: 01273 512186.*

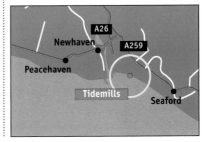

HAMBLE COMMON
Hampshire

■ *This mark consists of a shingle beach lying just west of the Hamble estuary on the Solent.*

Like most beaches in this area, it fishes best on spring tides at two-and-a-half hours either side of high water. Best fishing comes between autumn and January, but April is good.

SPECIES
The main species here are flounder, bass and silver eel, with a chance of hefty spring plaice to over 3lb. The summer produces eel with a lot of crabs and weed.

BEST BAIT
Rag is the best all-round bait to use, but peelers also have their moments. Silver eel are especially fond of peelers. Having a moving bait will bring a good response from flounder, while adding a couple of fluorescent beads or bright sequins will pay off.

TACKLE
The shingle beach at this mark is sheltered, and has only modest tides, so plain leads between 3oz-5oz will cope with anything less than a gale. Most flounder are taken close in, but plaice stay a little further out. A one-up, one-down rig with size 2 Aberdeens will be effective.

GETTING THERE
Leave the M27 at junction 8 and take the B3397 towards Hamble. Hamble Common is signposted as a right turn in Hamble village and a narrow road runs to the sea. There is a car park near the harbour entrance.

TACKLE SHOP
● *Sammy's Fishing Tackle & Baits, Cabin Boat Yard, Bursledon, Tel: 02380 406378.*

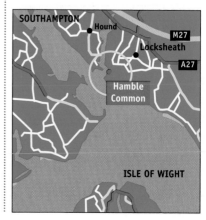

■ *The Hurst Shingle Bank stretches one-and-a-half miles east from Milford-on-Sea. The bank offers protection from every wind direction, which is a real bonus during the winter.*

The tidal race around the headland is very strong and this can be a problem when there is a lot of weed about.

SPECIES
Winter at this mark produces cod, with good flounder in the main river channel and backwater. Summer sees the best bass, mullet and ray. The river mouth and main channel are your best bet for specimen fish.

Hurst Hole offers conger, cod and bass, and is usually best in the autumn. The Castle Reach has deep water within easy casting range, where ray, cod, bass and flounder can all be taken.

BEST BAITS
Try almost anything from king ragworms and sandeels to squid, lugworms and peeler crabs. Fresh mackerel for the bass and conger.

TACKLE
The long walk to this mark can be a problem, so keep tackle to a minimum and travel light. Strong tides mean you will need to use 5oz or 6oz grip leads, so use a standard beachcaster capable of casting such weights.

GETTING THERE
Situated on the B3058 coastal road, the castle is a one-and-a-half mile walk along the shingle bank. However, rather than starting from Milford-on-Sea, you can drive down New Lane which cuts about 400 yards off the walk.

TACKLE SHOP:
● *Forest Sports & Tackle, 23b High St, Milford, Tel: 01590 643366.*

LEE-ON-THE-SOLENT
Hampshire

■ *This is a small resort with some panoramic views over the Solent. It offers a mile-and-a-half of shingle beach from Hill Head to Elmore Point.*

Best results are on night tides when fishing three hours before until two hours after high tide. Tides are moderate and the average spring tide is around 4.7 metres.

SPECIES
Target species include bass, plaice, smooth-hound, thornback ray, mackerel and dogfish in summer. Flounder, pouting and whiting are caught in the winter and early spring.

BEST BAIT
Use ragworms, peeler crabs, mackerel or squid.

TACKLE
A 12ft-13ft beachcaster is ideal for casting 4oz-6oz leads on 15lb-20lb mainline. Terminal rigs are normally one-up, one-down or one-up, two-down paternosters.

GETTING THERE
Come off the M27 at Fareham and you find the town. Car parking is located along the sea front, while there are other dedicated car parks.

TACKLE SHOP
● *South Coast Tackle, 179 High St, Lee-on-the-Solent, Tel: 01705 550209.*

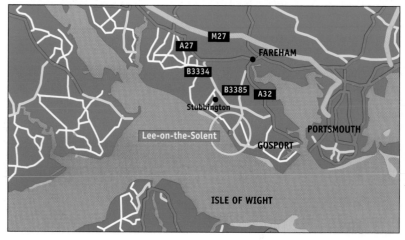

■ *This is a shallow beach in the attractive setting of the New Forest shoreline of the Solent. The best fishing is during the last three hours of the flood tide, with springs preferred to neaps.*

Lepe is surrounded by excellent smoothhound marks and has all the qualifications to produce the species in summer.

SPECIES
Best fishing is in the autumn and winter with flounder the main species. Bass and a few good cod are also caught. Late spring signals the return of the flounder, quickly joined by bass and silver eel.

BEST BAITS
Worms, with rag preferred to lug. Peeler crabs are useful, especially for eel and bass.

TACKLE
Standard beach gear is adequate with either plain or breakout leads; 5oz is enough unless there is a gale blowing. This is mainly a small fish beach, so size 1 or 2 Aberdeens are ideal. Long casts are not needed here, particularly around high water, when a short lob can find fish in the backwash.

GETTING THERE
From the M271, follow the A35 for Lyndhurst, turning off to the A326 towards Fawley. Then follow the signs for the Lepe Country Park. There is plenty of parking available.

TACKLE SHOP
● *Bell's Sports, 9-10 New Rd, Hythe, Tel: 02380 842065.*

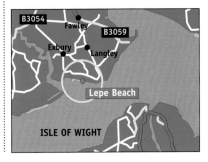

SOUTHSEA
Hampshire

■ *This steeply-sloping shingle beach runs onto sand around the low-water mark and is bounded by South Parade pier to the east and the castle to the west.*

SPECIES

Daytime in spring gives flounder, plaice and occasional bass. Silver eel arrive in May, with evening tides best. Summer is poor, but from late August there are sole.

Night tides in autumn and winter give pouting,

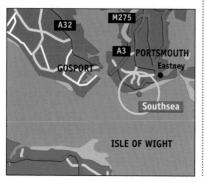

whiting, dab, flounder, eel and school bass.

BEST BAITS

Ragworms are the standard bait and catch all species. Peeler crabs are good for silver eel. Lugworms, white rag and peelers will catch better plaice. Dab like small pieces of fish, including sprat and kipper.

TACKLE

Standard beach gear with 15lb mainline is ideal for this clean beach. There is a strong lateral tide for a couple of hours each side of high tide on springs, demanding breakout leads.

A one-up, one-down rig with size 2 to 1/0 Aberdeen hooks works well, though a 4ft flowing trace of 15lb line scores with spring plaice.

GETTING THERE

Take the M275 to Portsmouth and follow the brown tourist signs to the Pyramids. Car parking is available there and on the seafront road.

TACKLE SHOP

● *Dave's Tackle, 1 The Precinct, South St, Gosport, Tel: 02392 529107.*

■ *This is a long shingle beach giving way to a shallow mix of mud and sand. It is on Southampton Water, east of the River Itchen and is a popular match venue.*

SPECIES

Flounder are caught for much of the year, but April and October to January produce the best catches. Silver eel, small bass and mullet are caught in summer.

BEST BAITS

Ragworms are the best bait. Several small worms often fish better than a large king rag.

TACKLE

Weston is sheltered, so a light beach rod with a 3oz-5oz plain lead is ideal and allows small fish to make their presence felt. Too light a lead will not cast multi-hook rigs very far, although most flounder are within 80 yards.

A one-up, one-down rig armed with size 2 Aberdeen hooks is good.

GETTING THERE

Leave the M27 at junction 8 and take the B3397 towards Hamble. Then take a right from the A3025 towards Woolston. Weston is signposted to the left.

TACKLE SHOP

● *Sammy's Fishing Tackle & Baits, Cabin Boat Yard, Bridge Rd, Bursledon, Tel: 02380 406378.*

BEMBRIDGE HARBOUR
Isle of Wight

■ There are two rocky areas on either side of the harbour - one to the north of St Helens and the other east of the lifeboat station. Both these produce wrasse and bass. Best fishing is on the flooding tide.

Fishing into the harbour from Bembridge or at St Helens produces flounder and silver eel. If you fish Bembridge, cast into the main channel which feeds the harbour.

SPECIES
Summer and autumn are best for the bass, eel and wrasse, but flounder can be caught at virtually any time.

BEST BAIT
Ragworms for flounder and rag/peeler crab cocktail for eel. Rag or crabs for wrasse. Bass like a big crab, fish bait or mackerel head and guts.

TACKLE
Standard beach gear will cope, but you may need a reel loaded with 30lb line for the rockier marks. A simple paternoster or running leger rig, with both carrying size 2 to 1/0 Aberdeen hooks for the flounder and eel.

If you are fishing the rockier marks on the other side of the harbour, you will need stronger gear. Hooks, such as Mustad Vikings, in sizes 1/0

to 3/0 catch wrasse, while size 4/0 to 6/0 hooks are safer for bass.

GETTING THERE
Reach St Helens by turning right on to the B3330 from Brading and drive past the village green. The road turns sharply to the left, turn right here along the narrow road to the Duver. There is ample parking. Bembridge is signposted from the B3330.

TACKLE SHOP
● *Screaming Reel, 55 St John's Rd, Ryde, Tel: 01983 568745.*

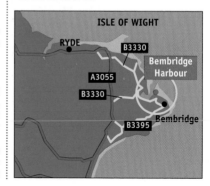

84

BEST BAITS
Good-quality frozen or fresh sandeels should be used for the ray, but strips of mackerel or pieces of pouting can be effective. Lugworms tempt the smaller fish, while crabs work for wrasse. Other species are taken on baits meant for ray.

TACKLE
Standard beach gear is fine but use 18lb-22lb mainline because of the snaggy sea bed. The big ray are caught between March and June.

Rigs should be a single-hook paternoster or a running leger with strong, size 2/0-4/0 hooks. Lure fishing and float work tempts bass. Mackerel often venture close to the shore in summer, so it's worth taking a set of feathers with you.

GETTING THERE
Park at the Whale Chine car park on the A3055. Access to the beach is down steep steps and along tricky cliff paths.

TACKLE SHOP
● *Screaming Reel, 55 St John's Rd, Ryde, Tel: 01983 568745.*

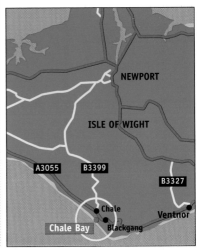

■ *This shingle beach stretches for over a mile along the Back of the Wight. It is noted for quality ray fishing, which is best when there is some colour in the water and a good sea running, during or just after a blow.*

SPECIES
Ray, along with big bass, pouting, dogfish, and occasional turbot, cod or conger eel.

■ *The five-mile long tidal section of the River Medina runs from Newport to Cowes, where it joins the Solent. The river is popular for flounder between October and January.*

The upper section from Newport to Stag Lane dries to a trickle at low water, exposing large expanses of thick mud, so fishing is only possible either side of high water.

Further downstream, the river is deeper and wider, but a low-water session will still require a trek across the mudflats. Both the flood and ebb tides can fish well, but the two hours or so of slack water is less productive.

SPECIES
The fishing is for flounder, mullet, bass and silver eel.

BEST BAITS
Fish two or three small ragworms to a hook for flounder or plaice. Mullet like a small Mepps spoon baited with ragworms or you can take float-fished bread.

TACKLE
Most anglers use standard beach gear with a two-hook running leger or spreader boom for flounder. A third hook is often added above the main trace as a flier to search out fish feeding closer to shore. Plaice can be taken between

Kingston power station and Cowes harbour using the same tactics.

The upper section at Newport quay is a popular spot for spinning for thin-lipped mullet. The thick-lipped variety are common in the lower section in and around Cowes harbour.

GETTING THERE
Access to Newport quay is off Quay Street, close to the town centre. The west bank can be reached by leaving the A3020 at Dodnor industrial estate or Stag Lane. The lane to Island harbour off the A30543 or Folly Lane off the A3021 gives access to the east bank.

TACKLE SHOP
● *Screaming Reel, 55 St John's Rd, Ryde, Tel: 01983 568745.*

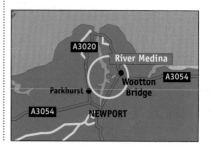

■ This pier offers the chance of various species and the opportunity to use a variety of techniques. A permit is required to here and they are available from the pier master.

Results are usually best at night, but there have been some very good fish landed in daylight. Fishing into the deep water at the pier's end is favoured by most locals.

There is unrestricted fishing day and night, except that no fishing is allowed on the north side between 6pm and 8pm on Wednesdays, because of boating activity. At the time of going to press, day tickets were £2.25, with half price concessions. Power casting styles are restricted.

SPECIES

Mackerel, black bream, pollack, eel, garfish, flatfish, school bass and smoothhound during summer, with cod in winter. Pouting and dogfish are caught all year.

BEST BAITS

Crabs or worms for smoothhound and squid for cod. Worms are the best all-round bait from the stem, but crabs can be effective. Smoothhound will take squid or hermit crabs.

TACKLE

The tide run is hard, even on a neap tide, so a 6oz grip lead is needed when casting off the front. The tide is particularly strong during the ebb. Tackle needs to be strong if you intend to go for the smoothhound or cod in the fast tide. Use size 4/0 Viking pattern hooks for hound. The stem should be fished by casting out westwards into the ferry channel or eastwards over a large shingle bank that dries at low water.

For some light tackle enjoyment, try spinning among the pier pilings with ragworm or lures. Alternatively, try float fishing off the front.

GETTING THERE

Yarmouth is approached on the A3054 or A3055. Access to the pier is at the entrance situated in the town square. There is limited parking.

TACKLE SHOP

● *Screaming Reel, 55 St John's Rd, Ryde, Tel: 01983 568745.*

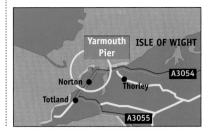

■ *This mark is a popular holiday area during the summer, but late evenings and night tides will also produce fish.*

Although this is a great spot, the hike down the cliffs is very exhausting – it's definitely not a trip for the faint-hearted. Summer and autumn provide the best sport.

SPECIES
Bass, conger and bull huss at night in summer, with small pollack and wrasse in daylight.

BEST BAITS
Mackerel fillets or whole squid are best for the bull huss and conger, while smaller mackerel baits and peeler crabs will sort out the bass. Crabs and ragworms work well for the wrasse.

TACKLE
The ground is extremely rough here, so a rotten-bottom rig is the only serious choice. All the species require big, strong hooks, such as a size 6/0 O'Shaughnessy, and equally strong trace line of at least 40lb.

The good news is that you only need to cast around 50 yards to be among the fish. Try to catch a small live pouting after dark and fish it on a hair rig for the bass and conger.

GETTING THERE
Durdle Door can be reached by hiking along the coastal path from Lulworth Cove or by parking at the holiday camp, where a small charge is made.

TACKLE SHOP
● *Purbeck Angling, 28 South St, Wareham, Tel: 01929 550770.*

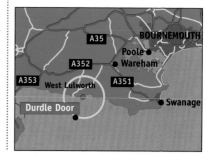

■ *This is an easily accessible and shallow, sandy beach to the west of Highcliffe, stretching about one mile to Steamer Point at the eastern end of Avon beach.*

Fishing over slack water gives the best results, although a good bass can be caught in rough conditions at any state of the tide.

SPECIES
Autumn seems to give the best sport at this mark, with sole, whiting, eel, bass, flounder, odd plaice, pouting and rockling. Rising night tides produce the best sport.

BEST BAITS
A lug/rag cocktail or blast frozen sandeel will catch bass. Otherwise stick to the obvious baits like peeler crabs and lugworms. Whiting like lug tipped with a slither of mackerel.

Lugworms take small bass, while mackerel fillet, sandeels or peelers take the bigger fish.

TACKLE
Use a three-hook paternoster rig for most species. Two hooks above is as good as any combination. It can pay to use one hook clipped down in calm or rough conditions. Rough conditions can give a good bass to a single, clipped-down rig.

Breakout leads are necessary. Weed sometimes causes a problem in early summer.

GETTING THERE
Follow the A337 from either Lymington or Christchurch. Turn into Bure Lane and then Southcliff Road. This brings you to Streamer Point car park.

TACKLE SHOP
● *Pro-Fishing Tackle, 258 Barrack Rd, Christchurch, Tel: 01202 484518.*

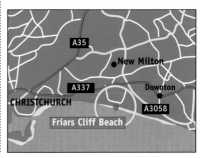

89

■ *A protective groyne was built on the south-east corner of the Hengistbury Head, its purpose to stem erosion. This spit, officially called Long Groyne, stretches out 200 yards and has become a major angling feature.*

Daybreak sessions are favoured, especially after a few days of settled weather. A south-westerly blow colours the water and reduces sport. Deep-water fishing is possible from half tide up for a variety of seasonal species. Float angling is best from the last four hours of the flood and the first two of the ebb.

Do not fish on the groyne in anything other than calm conditions. Waves swamp the venue in rough weather, so stick to the beach in a swell.

SPECIES
Winter produces cod, pouting, strap conger and rockling. Bass, mullet, ballan wrasse, plaice, pollack, dab, flounder and conger are the summer and autumn targets.

BEST BAITS
Peeler crab and ragworm are best for bottom fishing, while sandeel or mackerel slithers are best when using a float.

TACKLE
Legering, float fishing and spinning are all possible from the groyne. There is a fast tide at the end of the groyne and rough patches on clean ground, which suit float work during the flood. Bottom fishing should be on the east side during the flood tide, and therefore the west when it is ebbing.

GETTING THERE
Take the A35 from Christchurch or Bournemouth and the B3059 to Southbourne, following the signs to Hengistbury Head.

The headland groyne is reached by ferry from Mudeford Quay to a landing station in front of a long row of beach huts. From here it is a 10-minute walk. Alternatively you can take the land train, operating in summer, from the car park on the edge of the headland. The land train trip takes about 12 minutes.

From Hengistbury car park, you can take a footpath through fields and walk along the beach.

TACKLE SHOP
● *Pro-Fishing Tackle, 258 Barrack Rd, Christchurch, Tel: 01202 484518.*

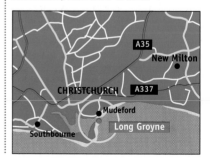

■ *Some of the biggest flounder from Poole Harbour are caught in daylight at Jerry's Point between Christmas and February.*

Remember that Poole Harbour has four tides in every 12 hours, there is a lot more tidal movement. Spring tides are best.

SPECIES
Eel and school bass dominate for most of the year, meaning that few anglers fish here until the flounder show.

BEST BAITS
Ragworms are best. Do not neglect slipper limpets, because a cocktail with rag can be the difference between catching and blanking.

TACKLE
Three-hook rigs, such as two above the lead and one below, with 12in snoods are the norm. Use a size 1 long-shank pattern hook.

Plain 3oz or 4oz lead weights are all you need and distance casting is not required. Good flounder are caught from as little as 30 yards. A few turns of the reel handle every now and then will also enhance your chances. Float fishing from the point during a south-westerly wind can produce a fish or two.

GETTING THERE
The ferry will take you across from the Sandbanks peninsula. Drive past the toll and carry on up the road until you come to a gate. Follow the track to the point.

If you are travelling from the west, take the road to Swanage from Wareham and turn left opposite Corfe Castle. This takes you to Studland. Follow the road until it straightens and you see the harbour on your left, then look for the gate.

TACKLE SHOP
● *Advanced Angling, 499 Christchurch Rd, Boscombe, Tel: 01202 303402.*

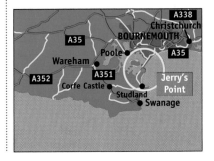

91

■ *This mark is situated between Weymouth Bay and Lulworth Cove. It offers a variety of species throughout the year.*

The bay has a secluded shingle beach with some ridges and reefs close in that attract fish. Situated in a National Trust area, this beach is busy in summer so is best avoided during the busy daylight hours.

Although you can fish under most conditions, the early part of the flood can be productive. June though to November is considered the most popular time. Beware of weed that can be a problem after storms.

SPECIES
Bass, wrasse, conger, pouting, rockling, pollack, ray and plaice.

BEST BAITS
Ragworms and peeler crabs are best, but squid, fish, lugworms and shellfish can be used.

TACKLE
Normal beachcasting methods are favoured, using a standard rod and reel combination, but float tactics or spinning can get results.

GETTING THERE
From the A35 at Dorchester, take the A352 towards Warmwell and then the A353 through Poxwell. Then take the left-hand turn up Upton from where the road leads to Ringstead Bay.

TACKLE SHOP
● **Purbeck Angling, 28 South St, Wareham, Tel: 01929 550770.**

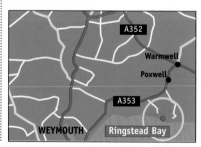

SOUTHBOURNE
Dorset

■ *This is the venue where the British record shore-caught plaice was caught. It is a shallow, sandy beach about three miles west of Hengistbury Head and offers an assortment of species throughout the year.*

Fish the full run up on midnight high waters or two hours up and two down for the best action.

SPECIES

Summer through to autumn produces sole after dark. Plaice, mackerel and odd pollack are caught in summer on a rising tide at dusk. Night tides give soles, bass, ray, pouting and dab. Small whiting, flounder, rockling, plaice, turbot and gurnard also feature.

This venue is not particularly productive in winter, except for small flounder and rockling.

BEST BAITS

A peeler crab tipped with ragworms will catch larger fish. Razorfish, slipper limpet with yellowtail lug, and ragworm cocktails are good for sole and most species from August to November. Frozen sandeels produce turbot, ray, bass, pollack and gurnard in daylight. A fillet or whole small pout also catch ray and bass at night. Fish baits catch odd ray, gurnard, dab and small whiting.

TACKLE

A Pennell rig on a long, single trace will produce ray, turbot, bass and even jumbo mackerel occasionally. After dark, a 60-yard cast will be far enough for sole in flat calm conditions. Size 2 or 4 hooks on paternoster rigs get results. A slow retrieve can produce results on a rising tide.

Breakout leads are needed during spring tides. Dab tend to be caught at distance, even in darkness. Most bottom rigs are effective, such as a one-up, one-down pattern.

Rolling surfs produce double-figure bass from the gutter during strong, windy conditions or immediately after.

GETTING THERE

Head for the Southbourne coast road, which runs along from Boscombe (Overcliff Drive) to Hengistbury Head. You will see that there is parking available, as well as access to the beach near Grange Road.

TACKLE SHOP

● *Advanced Angling, 499 Christchurch Rd, Boscombe, Tel: 01202 303402.*

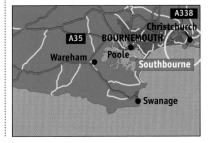

■ *This pier offers easy access with no step, which makes it popular, but there is also provision for novice divers so watch out for them.*

March and April are the months for rockling, pollack, wrasse, dogfish, flounders and odd plaice. The full run up the tide tends to fish best, with daylight as good as darkness.

There are landing stages either side for boats, so beware of the moorings.

Normally there are no restrictions, but, in 2002, the lower deck at the end had been closed due to storm damage.

SPECIES
Small wrasse, scorpion fish, plaice, pollack, smelt, bass and flounder in daylight. At night, it is dogfish, rockling pout, pollack, bass, odd ray, flounder and conger throughout the year.

May to September will give odd good bass, whiting and sometimes codling.

BEST BAITS
Ragworms are the top bait, although peeler crabs can do well. Frozen sandeels, mackerel and fresh pout strip will produce good fish. Squid will catch, but mackerel tends to be better in darkness, if you want a big fish.

Pollack will fall to a single ragworm as the tide floods, usually from April onwards. Fishing with a mackerel fillet bait on a Pennell rig in October and November can produce a good conger eel around high water. Squid is a good bait if there are a few cod about, but they don't show every year.

TACKLE
Float tactics are good in summer for pollack. Use of two-hook paternoster rig, either two above the weight or one above and one below, for most species. It pays to fish straight down or just away from the pier with a single-hook rig.

It is not necessary to cast far, especially as the remains of the old pier supports hold fish. Small leads, shockleaders and an awareness of people around you are necessary when fishing this pier.

GETTING THERE
This is an easy venue to find. Follow the road to Swanage, either from the Chain Ferry at Sandbanks or take the scenic route via Wareham and Corfe Castle. In Swanage, follow the sings to Durlstone Country Park and the pier.

TACKLE SHOP
● *Purbeck Angling, 28 South St, Wareham, Tel: 01929 550770.*

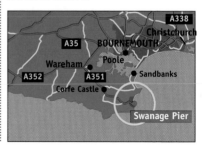

■ *Situated towards the western end of Chesil Beach, West Bexington, produces its best sport in big tides, although calm conditions are better for mackerel, garfish and flatfish.*

Coloured water after rough weather is better for whiting and codling. Best time is the last two hours of the flood and the first four of the ebb. Dusk to dark is best for sole and bass.

SPECIES

Noted for cod and whiting in winter, while plaice are the target in spring and summer. Plaice and dab show from March or April into summer. Sole appear from late summer.

Other summer species include mackerel and garfish, while bass can be around into late autumn. Expect dogfish, pouting, scad, poor cod, eel and smoothhound.

BEST BAITS

Lugworms take some beating here, but ragworms, peeler crabs, mackerel, sandeels and squid will also catch fish.

TACKLE

A beachcaster capable of handling grip weights up to 8oz is required due to the heavy tidal flow. Use two or three-hook paternoster rigs carrying fine-wire size 1-3/0 hooks for the flatfish and whiting. One or two-hook rigs carrying strong hooks up to size 6/0 are favoured for cod.

Although there is deep water within 40 yards, distance casting can be an advantage at times.

GETTING THERE

Take the B3157 from either Weymouth or Bridport. From the latter, you can follow the signs for Swyre, turning right on to a minor road opposite the pub. This road leads to West Bexington and then to the beach car park. From Weymouth, you travel towards Swyre but turn left to West Bexington, going straight over the crossroads to the beach car park.

TACKLE SHOP

● *The Tackle Shop (Potters), 9E West Bay, Bridport, Tel: 01308 428226.*

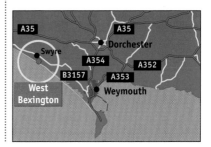

ALDERNEY BREAKWATER
Braye, Alderney, Channel Isles

■ *This Victorian breakwater is 1,609 yards long, but only 967 yards are visible. It stretches out on the northern side of Alderney at Braye and produces many species both summer and winter.*

More than 50 species have been recorded from the island, which is, at six square miles, the third largest of the Channel Islands and the most northerly. It is only nine miles from the French coast. A rising tide is generally productive.

SPECIES
The seasons at Alderney breakwater are October to April for mullet, August to December for garfish, September to December for conger and the big pollack, May to January for bass, November to January for tope, October to February for ray. Turbot and brill can be caught all year round.

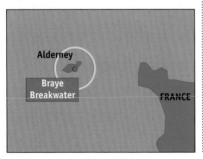

BEST BAITS
Large squid, pouting and mullet make good bait for. Most baits are available, except peeler crabs and king ragworms. Bass, brill and turbot like live sandeels, but most baits work for the former. Rag will take mullet, while fish baits take tope, ray and pollack.

TACKLE
Fishing is into nearly 90 feet of water onto sand, but light-tackle tactics together with groundbait usually gets results, especially with the mullet and garfish. Big pollack also fall to float tactics.

Bass fall to most methods, including spinning. Conger take baits fished on the bottom; use 35lb minimum line and a 100lb leader.

Use a running leger for tope. Ray, brill and turbot are caught to beachcasting tactics, using fish baits in deep water. Make sure you've got a drop net.

GETTING THERE
From the capital of Alderney, St Anne, take the Route de Braye which takes you through Newtown and to Braye. You can't miss the breakwater to the north-west.

TACKLE SHOP
● *D&M Tackle & Sport, Queen Elizabeth II St, Alderney, Tel: 01481 824884.*

■ Gorey harbour in Jersey has to be one of the most beautiful locations in the British Isles to wet a line. The inner harbour is strewn with mooring ropes and is virtually impossible to fish, but the outer wall is very popular with local anglers.

Due to high levels of tourist activity during the daytime, most angling is done either at very first light, or in darkness.

The rocky outcrop at the rear of the castle can be fished low water up for species that come into the area to feed during quieter times. The rocks stretch around the coast in a northerly direction and are noted for plugging and spinning for bass.

Good catches of conger are taken from the rocks left of the slipway when fishing low water up at night; fish to 30lb are always likely. Flatfish are occasionally taken from the pier head.

The pier is very popular on winter evenings, with anglers jigging for squid under the lights and specimens to more than 4lb are often landed.

SPECIES
Bass, conger, mackerel, ray and squid.

BEST BAITS
Flatfish are caught on worms, with ray taking fish baits. Spinners and plugs are good for bass. Conger will take fish baits.

TACKLE
Use standard beachcasting gear at the pier head, but stronger tackle is required for the conger from the rocks. Use light spinning rods for plugging and for fishing squid jigs.

GETTING THERE
Take the A3 coast road from St Helier to Gorey, following the shoreline past Grouville Bay until the castle comes into view. There is parking available at the pier and in the village.

TACKLE SHOP
● *The Market Tackle Shop, 7 Beresford Market, St Helier, Tel: 01534 874875.*

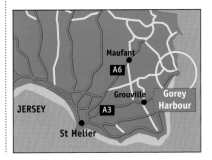

97

SOREL POINT
Jersey, Channel Isles

■ This north coast headland at this mark has a fierce tidal run that flows past the point and is famed locally for its mackerel fishing. Most anglers cast feathers and small spinners into the tide and retrieving at high speed.

Pollack and bass feed here and are often caught on artificial lures. Ballan wrasse inhabit the rough ground closer to shore and can reach specimen size; the best method for catching these is float fishing.

Bottom fishing can be hazardous due to the rough terrain, but anglers fishing with heavy tackle can expect to occasionally land ray, dogfish and conger.

SPECIES
Mackerel are the main species in spring and summer, with pollack and bass always possible. Wrasse can be excellent in the warmer months.

BEST BAITS
Feathers, small metal lures and spoons will take mackerel, with larger artificials best for pollack and bass. Most productive static baits are sandeels, squid and mackerel fillet. Green shore crabs and peelers are best for ballan wrasse.

TACKLE
Use light to medium spinning rods for fishing with lures. Choose a medium to heavy beachcasting rod and reel in the 7500-class for the bottom fishing.

GETTING THERE
Follow the A9 as far as St John's village, then turn right on to La Route du Nord (C101), which will take you past Ronez quarry. Once past the quarry, there is another right-hand turn which leads to the Sorel Point. There is enough space for a couple of cars close to the viewing point. From here you can take the short walk to the rock mark below.

TACKLE SHOPS
● *The Market Tackle Shop, 7 Beresford Market, St Helier, Tel: 01534 874875.*

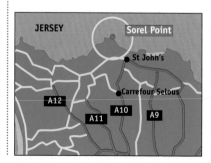

98

ST CATHERINE'S BREAKWATER
Jersey, Channel Isles

■ *One of the most famous shore marks in Jersey, the breakwater has produced specimens and British record fish.*

Its vast length means that it can accommodate many anglers on both the front and back wall, but there are specific hot spots.

The very end is popular with locals who feather for the summer mackerel, but also produces some big ray. The slip at the start of the breakwater is renowned for bass.

Because of the strong tidal run that affects the mark, most fishing is done during the slack water periods that precede and follow high and low water.

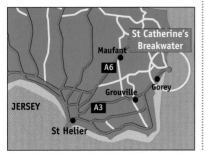

BAIT
Whole squid, mackerel strip, and small pouting mounted on pulley rigs work well for ray. Small green shore crabs under a float or legered close to the wall catch wrasse to specimen size.

TACKLE
Medium to heavy beachcasters are required to cast the heavy leads needed to place baits in the strong tide. The mixed ground calls for sturdy rig construction. A large drop-net is absolutely essential to land fish at any point on the wall.

GETTING THERE
From St. Helier, travel east on La Grand Route de la Cote as far as Gorey and stay on the main road up on over the headland above the castle. The breakwater will be seen in the distance as you follow the road. Stay on the coast road until you come to a right-hand turn to La Route de St Catherine, which will lead you to the car parking at the start of the wall.

TACKLE SHOP
● *The Market Tackle Shop, 7 Beresford Market, St Helier, Tel: 01534 874875.*

99

AXMOUTH
Devon

■ *Axbridge and Seaton lie at the mouth of the River Axe almost on the border between Dorset and Devon. The narrow inlet between the two offers excellent fishing for bass, codling, coalfish and whiting, to name but a few.*

The high shingle bank at the mouth of the river is the perfect position to cast into the middle of the channel.

SPECIES
Winter fishing at this mark offers codling, whiting and coalfish at night. High tide during those hot summer evenings often sees huge shoals of mackerel congregating within reasonable casting distance.

A flooding tide at night is the most popular time for catching the bass, which appear in May and are caught right through until late autumn. Conger eels can be caught at night from the rocky ground.

BEST BAITS
Peeler crabs, sandeels, ragworms and mackerel baits will all catch the bass. Other good baits to try for the mullet include tiny ragworms, mackerel flesh and bread flake. Conger eels will take large mackerel baits.

TACKLE
A simple beachcasting outfit is all you will need for most of the species, but lighter gear can be use. Bass and mackerel will accept bright lures

worked at speed. There are plenty of mullet to be caught on float fished maggots.

GETTING THERE
Axmouth is signposted off the A3052 Lyme Regis to Exeter road. Turn off at Colyford on to the B3172 to Axmouth, where you will see the small road bridge.

TACKLE SHOPS
● *The Tackle Box, 20 Marine Parade, The Cobb, Lyme Regis, Tel: 01297 443373.*
● *Exeter Angling Centre, Smythen St, Exeter, Tel: 01392 436404.*

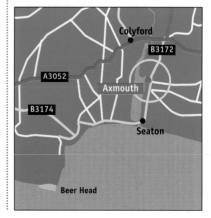

BRIXHAM BREAKWATER
Devon

■ Brixham's harbour is protected by a long breakwater that is well used by anglers.

The outside edge can be fished along its full length, but there are restrictions in the oil fuel jetty area, which faces the harbour. A flood tide coming to the high at about 7pm during late autumn is good, but calm weather is essential.

On the west side of the breakwater is Shoalstone beach, which gives bass, pollack and mackerel; best fishing is at dawn.

The lighthouse end is popular in summer, so there can be overcrowding, particularly during an evening flood tide when mackerel and garfish are in a feeding mood.

SPECIES
Conger, bass, pollack, plaice, dab, wrasse, whiting, pouting, mullet, mackerel and garfish.

BEST BAITS
Conger take mackerel, squid or small fish baits. Bread takes mullet, while worms or crabs work for other species. A live sandeel on float gear tempts bass. Crabs and ragworms take wrasse.

TACKLE
Mackerel will fall to float fished baits on size 2 hooks, feathers and spinning tactics. Conger accept fish baits on the bottom, while plaice, dab, pollack, wrasse, whiting and pouting are

also caught with bottom rigs. Summer mullet fishing is good when it is quiet. The inside edge of the marina tends to be better than the seaward side. Mullet are caught into the autumn and sometimes as late as November. Use a size 8 hook on a 4lb hooklength.

GETTING THERE
Take the A3022 from Paignton or A3122 from Dartmouth. Follow the signs to the marina and you can't miss the breakwater. There is ample parking near the breakwater, but it gets congested in summer.

TACKLE SHOP
● *Brixham Bait & Tackle, 10 The Quay, Brixham, Tel: 01803 853390.*

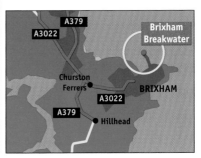

101

CHALLABOROUGH
Devon

■ This beach, just to the west of Bigbury-on-Sea and Burgh Island, produces bass and ray.

The ray season tends to start around May and slows down in November. Night tides on calm nights produce the best results.

SPECIES

All this stretch of coast is visited by small-eyed and spotted ray, along with an odd blonde ray in recent years. Conger eel also make an appearance from the westward end of the beach, where rocks extend towards the mouth of the River Erme.

Bass are caught during the first few hours of daylight and during dusk. Spring tides produce best, especially when there is a strong wind from the south and west whipping up a good surf.

BEST BAITS

Legered sandeels or launce, peeler crabs or worms, and crab/squid cocktails are all good choices for the bass.
Ray prefer live or frozen sandeel, and the conger eels like cuttlefish, squid or whole fish. A number of big bass have been landed here on squid head.

TACKLE

To fish from this mark, you will need a sturdy outfit capable of casting large baits some distance. A simple Pennell rig covers most options and helps when using bit baits.

GETTING THERE

Challaborough is reached by turning off the A379 towards the south-east of Modbury. Then take the B3392 to St Ann's Chapel, turn right and head for Ringmore. The beach is roughly two miles along this road.

TACKLE SHOP

● *Devon Angling Centre, Units 4/5, Orchard Meadow, Chillington, Kingsbridge, Tel: 01548 580888.*

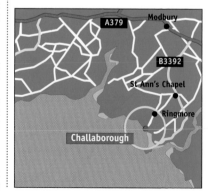

■ *The rugged foreshore under Plymouth Hoe is riddled with underwater caves which provide a perfect habitat for conger eel.*

The area is known as the Lion's Den, and is adjacent to the men-only bathing station. It is accessible at all states of the tide.

Best results here occur in calm conditions on small to medium height tides at night.

SPECIES
Conger, bass and wrasse.

BEST BAITS
Squid, cuttlefish, mackerel or small live pouting for conger. Live sandeels or crabs for bass.

TACKLE
A strong, standard beach rod with 7,000 size multiplier is best for conger to 50lb-class. Bass to 12lb take both bottom and float fished baits. Smaller reels can be used for bass and wrasse.

GETTING THERE
A one-way system operates on this part of the foreshore and it is reached via the Barbican and Citadel Road. The Lion's Den is just beyond the Royal Western Yacht Club on the left-hand side. Parking on the road is restricted until 6pm.

TACKLE SHOP
● *Manadon Angling Supplies, 11 St Eart, Rd, Manadon, Plymouth, 01752 795060.*

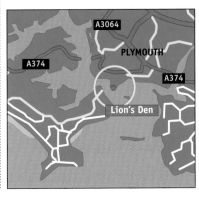

■ The area is one of the most picturesque in the South West and absolutely idyllic on a sunny afternoon when grey mullet cruise in the channels.

Bass come into the inlet at first light on a rising tide and at dusk. Night fishing from Fernycombe beach, which is the furthest out on the eastern flank, and Wonwell beach, closer in on the same side, yields ray and good sole are occasionally caught. On the western flank, Meadowsfoot beach is not open to anglers on Monday, Tuesday and Thursday.

Estuary mullet are very wily and the channel selected as the tide makes must be approached very quietly, then groundbaited.

SPECIES
Mullet, sole, thornback ray and small-eyed ray

BEST BAITS
Peeler crabs or soft crabs for thornback ray, but live prawns are best. A live or defrosted sandeel takes the majority of small-eyed ray. Sandeels, razorfish, squid and cuttlefish are often the basis of big cocktails for the bass.

Bread, maggots and pieces of a ragworm on a size 6 hook to a float rig.

TACKLE
A beachcaster and multiplier putting out a two-hook pulley rig is the preferred tactic.

GETTING THERE
Come off the A379 eight miles east of Plymouth and turn right at crossroads marked Holbeton. Carry on along narrow roads with passing places bringing you to Mothecome. Go under the Flete Estate Bridge and a few hundred yards on is the grass car park.

For the east side of the estuary, come off the A379 at crossroads joining the B3392. Go towards Kingston and from here the road is very narrow and the parking opportunities are limited to hedge pull-ins.

TACKLE SHOP
● *Devon Angling Centre, Units 4/5, Orchard Meadow, Chillington, Kingsbridge, Tel: 01548 580888.*

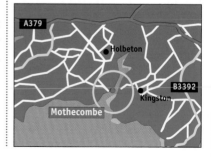

PRINCESS & HALDON PIERS
Torquay, Devon

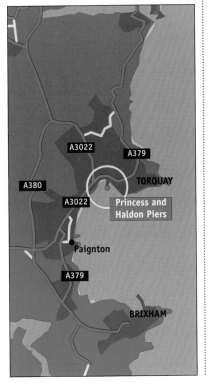

■ These two piers are really the guarding arms of the New Harbour in Tor Bay. Princess pier is on the west and Haldon pier faces it on the east. Angling is free from the outside-facing flanks and the ends of both piers, which have easy access close to Torquay's harbour area.

Early morning and evening fishing, ideally on a flooding tide, is productive throughout the summer and well into autumn.

SPECIES
Mackerel, mullet, garfish, dab, bass, plaice, flounder and eel in summer and autumn, with whiting, pouting and coalfish in winter.

BEST BAITS
Mackerel strip for mackerel and garfish. A small live sandeel or prawns for bass. Bread flake, mackerel flesh and maggots for mullet. Ragworms or pieces of crab for flatfish and eel.

TACKLE
Mackerel and garfish are mostly taken with a sliding float rig. Mullet can be coaxed within float range of the pier heads by groundbaiting. Dab, plaice, small flounder and silver eel are taken with bottom fishing tackle.

GETTING THERE
Head for the Torre Abbey Sands area of the seafront (Torbay Road) from where you can see Princess pier. This pier is on Princess Parade near the theatre, while Haldon pier is across the harbour on Victoria Parade.

TACKLE SHOP
● *Torbay Angling, 7 Dartmouth Rd, Paignton, Tel: 01803 552496.*

105

■ Seaton comprises a steeply-shelving shingle beach, giving way to cliffs and rough ground at either end. The harbour is situated at the east end of the beach.

Codling show from mid-November until late February to squid and lug cocktails are best. Night tides fish best with the first four hours of the rising tide the optimum.

Expect dogfish and bass most of the year, while the other main species can be caught from June to early October.

SPECIES

Dogfish, ray, bass, garfish, mackerel, pollack, wrasse, mullet and cod.

BEST BAITS

Squid, live or frozen sandeels, mackerel, black lug, peeler crabs and harbour ragworms.

TACKLE

A standard beachcaster and a 6500-size reel loaded with 15lb mainline is sufficient. Casts of 80-100 yards will put you among the fish. A 5oz grip lead will be needed as there is a strong lateral tide flow here.

Bass roam the beach and the entrance to the harbour, where a float-fished sandeel or legered live ragworm or peeler crab are the top baits. Summer mackerel and pollack fall to feathers and float fishing.

Try for mullet midway between the harbour mouth and mooring area, using a small spinner baited with harbour rag.

GETTING THERE

Follow the A3052 until you see the B3172 sign Axmouth and Seaton. Follow this road through Axmouth and take the first left after you have passed over the bridge. This road leads to the sea front where parking is plentiful.

TACKLE SHOPS

● *The Tackle Box, 20 Marine Parade/The Cobb, Lyme Regis, Tel: 01297 443373.*
● *Exeter Angling Centre, Smythen St, Exeter, Tel: 01392 436404.*

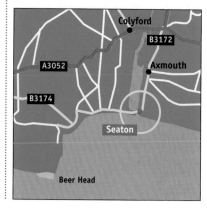

■ *Massive flounder are not as plentiful as they were, but this estuary remains the most productive area in Britain for flatties in the 3lb and over class. Catches of fish between to 2lb 8oz remains very high.*

The Teign is the venue for the National Flounder Championships in November when a minimum of 400 fish to 4lb always reach the scales. Conservation is practised and all are kept alive and returned to the water after weighing.

Specific areas give the better fish. The Shaldon flank has Gravel Point, Charlie's Beach and Coombe Cellars. The Teignmouth side has the Boatyard (two British records came from here), Flow Point, and the productive Red Rocks.

SPECIES
Exclusively flounder.

BEST BAITS
Peeler and soft crabs take most of the Teign's flatties. Ragworms achieve some success in the Netherton area, located at the top of the river near the motorway bridge.

TACKLE
Paternoster and pulley rigs and single hook running traces are punched out into the deep channel areas (easily identified at low water). It is best to fish the bottom of the tide up over high water and the first two hours of the back run.

GETTING THERE
The Teign (Teignmouth side) is signposted off the A380 at Kingsteignton roughly 11 miles from the M5 coming from Bristol. For the Shaldon side, carry straight on across the motorway bridge to Penn Inn roundabout. Go sharp left, signposted Milber, and carry straight on. The river is on your left. Coombe Cellars is the first mark of note.

TACKLE SHOP
● *Exeter Angling Centre, Smythen St, Exeter, Tel: 01392 436404.*

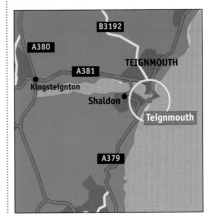

■ *This blockhouse mark on the south flank of the River Tamar offers sport for quality conger eel and thornback ray. Cod are caught in winter and the potential for other species is very good.*

This rugged venue is full of holes and indents that make it a haven for conger eel. If you are after the conger, fish from dusk into the night for best results.

Conger are caught throughout the year, but become docile in cold winters. Thornback ray are around between late April through to October.

SPECIES
Conger eel, thornback ray and cod.

BEST BAITS
For good results, squid and cuttlefish, small pouting and pollack for conger. Ray prefer fresh peeler crabs or softies

TACKLE
The nature of the bottom obviously takes its toll on tackle, so a sturdy, powerful beachcasting set up is required. Rotten-bottom rigs are a must and it is advisable to use heavier than normal line, for both mainline and traces.

GETTING THERE
Take the Plymouth to Torpoint car ferry and follow the A374 to Antony. Take the left fork at the pub signposted to Millbrook.

Carry on around the estuary to Mount Edgcumbe. There is plenty of foreshore to fish from a good car parking adjacent to Cremyll.

TACKLE SHOP
● *Millbrook Anglers, 100 West St, Millbrook, Torpoint, Tel: 01752 822216.*

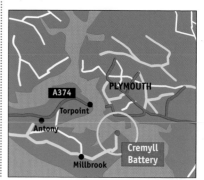

POLHAWN COVE
Cornwall

■ *The cove with its many deep gullies and heavy covering of kelp is on the right-hand side of the prominent Rame Headland.*

It fishes well throughout the summer and autumn for big wrasse. Mackerel and garfish show during the making tide and evening high water.

SPECIES
Ballan wrasse, conger eel, mackerel and garfish

BEST BAITS
Crabs, mackerel, squid, cuttlefish and lures.

TACKLE
A stiff-actioned beach rod and multiplier carrying 35lb mono is the best rig for the ballan wrasse that resist being dragged out of the hazardous bottom. A soft rod gives them far too much space to play with in the opening of the encounter.

Mackerel and garfish are taken with sliding float rig or by lure fishing when the tide is up. Use tough leger rig for conger, such as a 150lb trace of about 4ft carrying a size 10/0 hook.

GETTING THERE
From the A38 spine road coming off the Tamar Bridge, go to Trerulefoot then turn left on to the A374, which takes you to Antony. From there it is a narrow coast road via Tregantle, Freathy and Tregonhawke to Polhawn.

There is a reasonable amount of road and off-road parking on the cliff top. On no account must you use the private road leading to the fort to reach the waterline. Paths run down the cliff on the public side of the area.

TACKLE SHOP
● *The Tackle & Bait Shop, 93 Victoria Rd, St Budeaux, Plymouth, Tel: 01752 361294.*

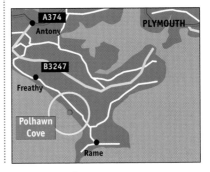

■ *Porthcurno has an interesting beach, with a fairly steep drop-off into deeper water near the low water mark.*

Although popular with holiday makers during the warmer months, early and late in the day anglers will have the beach to themselves, but some of the most interesting fishing is from the rocks under the Minack Theatre.

The first few hours of the flood tide is often the most productive period, especially after dark for the bass and ray.

SPECIES
Mackerel, garfish, scad, pollack, mullet, bass and wrasse from the rocks. Bass and occasional ray from the beach. The word is that occasional cod are caught in the colder months, along with coalfish, whiting and pouting.

BEST BAITS
Crabs, lugworms, ragworms and mackerel strip. Spinning and plugging will produce pollack, mackerel and bass from the rocks. Groundbaiting with mashed mackerel and bread mix will attract the mullet, mackerel and pollack.

TACKLE
Standard beach outfits for legering and heavy-duty spinning rods for float-fishing, spinning and plugging.

GETTING THERE
Take the A30 out of Penzance toward Land's End. At Catchall, take the B3283 following the signs for the Minack Theatre. There is a large car park with a path at the far end towards the beach.

TACKLE SHOP
● *Newtown Angling Centre, Germoe,* **Tel: 01736 763721.**

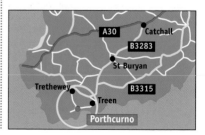

■ *This mark at the popular holiday resort of St Ives is best on a flowing tide from early flood to one hour's ebb, after which the ebb tides flows strongly to the west.*

At The Island, spring tides are more productive than neaps, with high water between 6pm and 9pm being the best.

SPECIES
Expect to catch garfish and mackerel in summer, along with plaice, flounder, turbot and even John Dory. Whiting and dogfish are caught after dark, especially in winter, as are dab.

BEST BAITS
Lugworms and ragworms take plaice, dab, whiting, wrasse and other bottom feeders, although whiting also take mackerel strip and sandeels. The latter can be used on float gear to take garfish. Mackerel are caught when spinning with a sandeel or a set of tinsels.

TACKLE
Light tackle can be used here, particularly in summer, particularly for spinning and float fishing. Winter sport requires a standard beachcasting outfit. Two and three-hook paternoster rigs are favoured.

GETTING THERE
This mark is at the northern end of St Ives and identified by St Nicholas' Chapel on the western side of the summit and the former Coastguard station to the east.

Take the A30 to the west end of the Hayle bypass, turn right towards Lelant on the A3074 to St Ives.

At St Ives, follow the one-way system around the harbour to Porthgwidden car park. Take the coastal footpath to the top of The Island on the left of the old Coastguard station. Turn left and then right onto the path leading to the mark.

TACKLE SHOP
● *Tim's Tackle, 2 The Wharf, St Ives, Tel: 01736 795329.*

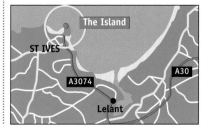

■ *Although the bottom consists of mainly heavy kelp beds, there are several productive deep gullies under the rod tip.*

This area fishes best from May to November, although good catches of wrasse have been taken in January.

SPECIES
Wrasse, pollack, mackerel, garfish, mullet and conger.

BEST BAITS
Ragworms and lugworms catch wrasse and small pollack, while mackerel or sandeels can be used to catch other species.

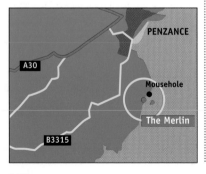

TACKLE
Fishing a freelined worm under the rod tip for wrasse and pollack on light tackle. It is best over low water and the first two hours of the flood. The gully nearest to the cove can be fished from two hours up to high water using the same methods.

Float fish for wrasse and pollack over the second half of the flood. Mackerel and garfish are taken over high water spring tides.

Long casting from the Bible Rock over high water puts legered worms on to a soft bottom at least 70 yards off. Use rotten-bottom links to cut tackle losses.

GETTING THERE
Take the A30 to Penzance and follow the coast road to Mousehole. Park in the car park next to or on the South pier. It is possible to walk along the shore over low water and up to half tide to reach the Merlin area. The alternative over the top half of the tide is to walk part of the way up Raginnis Hill from the church before taking the first footpath on the seaward side, just before the double garage.

TACKLE SHOP
● *Jim's Discount Tackle, 59a Causewayhead, Penzance, Tel: 01736 360159.*

TREYARNON BAY
Cornwall

■ This is a narrow sandy beach, on North Cornwall's Atlantic coast, is flanked by rocks and swept by vicious currents.

You can catch bass nearly all year, but realistically between May and December. Gentle to medium onshore conditions will see bass move in to mop up any food.

SPECIES
Bass, wrasse and pollack.

BEST BAITS
Use either large peeler crab baits, lugworms or live sandeels.

TACKLE
Use one rod, travel light and fish at night. Do not use a tripod when bass fishing. There is no need for distance casting

Remember to keep any light off the water and keep noise to a minimum. You can also go plugging all around here during the day.

If you follow the cliff path left of the beach you will come to some tall cliffs. Look around because there are a couple of places where it is safe to get down to the wrasse-holding ground. Although caught by traditional tactics, it can be fun to float-fish with lighter gear, if the water is relatively calm. Old crabs and worms can be mashed up and thrown in for groundbait.

Bass can also be caught here, both to legering and plugging.

GETTING THERE
Follow signs from Padstow for St Merryn and go through the village. Look for a signpost on the right to Treyarnon Bay. The road is very narrow. Park in the car park below the hotel and pay the small fee if someone is there to collect it.

The beach is on your left as you approach the car park. Walk left around the beach, via the cliff path, until you come to a wooden bench overlooking gently sloping rocks exposed around low water.

TACKLE SHOP
● *Bude Angling Supplies, 6 Queens St, Bude, Tel: 01288 353396.*

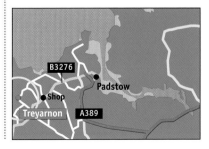

■ *Aust is a South Gloucestershire village closest to the old Severn Bridge, on the English side of the Bristol Channel.*

For 200 yards either side of the bridge, and indeed directly underneath, there is great potential for sea anglers. This is a low-water mark though, which can only be tackled when the tide is on the way out.

Aust rock supports the bridge and is situated just under and to the right of the bridge. It runs out for around 200 yards. This is rough ground and tackle losses can be heavy.

SPECIES
Codling, conger, whiting, pouting, flounder, dab, silver eel, shad, occasional bass and mullet are caught under the bridge. Conger and cod get the most interest.

BEST BAITS
Lugworms, ragworms, squid, peeler crabs and mackerel are the best baits.

TACKLE
Rigs are mostly basic paternoster Pennell rigs. Pulley rigs are useful on rough ground. Fixed-grip lead can be useful on the sand and mud. Mustad Nordic Bend or Viking hooks in size 2/0 to 4/0 are favoured for cod and conger. Aberdeen hooks in size 1 or 2 sort out the flatfish and silver eel. Use 15lb mainline and a suitable shockleader for 4oz-6oz lead weights, which are needed in the fast-flowing water.

GETTING THERE
The M48 crosses the old Severn Bridge, but take the A403 (junction 1) to Aust. There is a long walk which can be a pain in winter, and anglers should be wary of the rising tide creeping in behind them.

TACKLE SHOP
● *Veals & Sons Ltd, 61 Old Market St, Bristol, Tel: 0117 926 0790.*

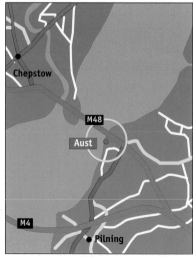

■ This mark is a rocky peninsula that juts out into the Bristol Channel, just south of Weston-super-Mare. Big fish feed close in here and, over the years, there have been numerous big cod, conger eel and bass.

The north side is favoured by local anglers, although very dangerous if you're not familiar with it and lethal during darkness.

High water during spring tides gives the best results with two hours up and one-and-a-half hours down the top time.

SPECIES

In winter you can expect cod, whiting, flounder, pouting and dogfish. The summer gives ray, conger eel, some large bass and silver eel.

BEST BAITS

King ragworms and lugworms will sort out the winter codling and whiting, while peeler crabs and whole squid will help take the bass and conger eels.

TACKLE

A cast of no more than 30 yards puts you among the fish. Fishing on the mud allows your tackle to roll with the tide to the rocks situated just 20 yards out.

This is where the fish forage for crabs and shellfish that live among the rocks and weed.

Use 30lb mono straight through, with an 8oz lead advisable to combat the strong lateral currents and rough ground.

Make sure you use some form of rotten bottom on your rig.

GETTING THERE

Head out of Weston-super-Mare on the Burnham road, turn right at the Anchor pub and Brean Down is signposted from here. To get to the top you must climb from the south side which is signposted from Brean Village.

TACKLE SHOP

● *Chris's Angling Centre, 12 Regent St, Burnham, Tel: 01278 794442.*

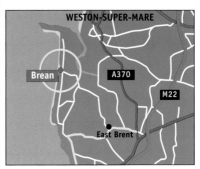

CLEVEDON
Somerset & Gloucester

■ *The sea front provides fishing from a number of rock stations and the low-water reefs offer cod in autumn and winter.*

There is no need for distance casting over this mixed ground of small rocks, mud and sand. Two hours either side of the top is best.

SPECIES
Expect sport with conger, thornback ray, sole, dogfish, dab and silver eel in summer, with whiting, pouting and cod during autumn and winter. Bass are a bonus catch.

BEST BAITS
King ragworms are best. Lugworms are popular for cod, when bunched on a size 4/0 hook and tipped with a strip of squid. Mackerel and small whole squid will take conger, ray and sometimes cod. Thin strips of mackerel will tempt the bigger whiting.

TACKLE
Strong tackle is advised here (use a minimum 25lb line) with size 4/0-plus hooks. Gear is reduced for the flatfish and whiting, and size 1 hooks are recommended.

Despite the use of grip leads with long wires,

it can be difficult to hold bottom when spring tides are in flow.

GETTING THERE
Take junction 20 off the M5, following the slip road signposted to Clevedon. Cross both roundabouts, go left at the traffic lights and directly west to reach the sea front. There is a car park opposite the pumphouse mark, or turn right for the bandstand.

TACKLE SHOP
● *The Tackle Box, Station Rd, Clevedon, Tel: 01275 340180.*

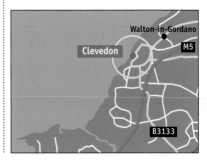

116

■ *This is a low water venue next to Hinkley Point power station on the Bristol Channel coast. Fishing is from broken ground between the power station and Stolford.*

Tides from 9.5 metres to 11.5 metres offer the best potential, when fishing three hours down and two hours up.

SPECIES
Hinkley can provide some brilliant cod sport between October to March with 20lb fish possible. Other winter species include whiting, dogfish, sole and pouting. Summer species include bass, ray, conger and flatfish.

BEST BAITS
King ragworms and lugworms sort out the winter codling. Whole squid produces the bigger cod from December through to January. Rag, crabs and mackerel tempt bass and ray.

TACKLE
Distance casting is fundamental on the initial part of the ebbing tide, but cut back on the start of the new flood.

A cast of 120yd or more will yield double-figure cod, whiting and thornback ray. Casting close in produces conger eel, bass and silver eel.

A rotten-bottom rig is advisable when fishing at short range. Pennell pulley rigs are best.

GETTING THERE
Access to Hinkley Point is by turning off the M5 at junction 24 and taking the Bridgewater road to Cannington. The road to the point is signposted down to the power station.

Park in the visitors' car park and walk down the footpath to the cliff top. Then follow the footpath along the cliff-top and drop down on to the reefs.

TACKLE SHOP
● *Wayne's Tackle, 61 Eastover, Bridgwater, Tel: 01278 429335.*

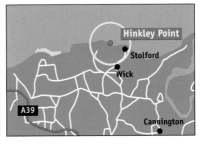

117

■ *The foreshore provides fishing from a number of marks from the edge of Battery Point along the sea front to the sailing club.*

The favoured mark is behind the swimming pool at the base of the steps leading up to Battery Point. Fishing over high water on spring tides gives the best sport. Try fishing one-and-a-half hours up and two hours down.

SPECIES

It is possible to catch cod, whiting, dab and flounder in winter, while the summer will produce sole, eel, odd ray, small conger and school bass.

Codling are prominent from October through to April. Congers are evident from May until October and it is quite possible for the eel to stay even longer if the weather remains mild.

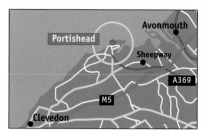

BEST BAITS

Mackerel strip will take whiting, while peeler crabs and rag cocktails will catch codling. Peeler crabs will take codling, while rag and lug baits catch flounder and dab. A cocktail of mackerel and herring cast close in among the rocks will produce conger.

TACKLE

There is a strong, lateral left to right tidal flow towards high water. Casting up tide and letting your tackle trot round towards the edge of Battery Point is a very good method.

Fish will venture up the side of the point, to feed on the shrimps and crabs which frequent the rocks and mud there. A longer cast during rough conditions will put you among the cod and whiting.

Short casts with two-hook flapper rigs will produce dab, flounder, bass and silver eel.

GETTING THERE

Portishead foreshore is reached by leaving junction 19 off the M5 and following the signs for the sea front.

TACKLE SHOP

● *Veals & Sons Ltd, 61 Old Market St, Bristol, Tel: 0117 926 0790.*

SAND POINT
Weston-super-Mare, Somerset & Gloucester

■ *The rocky headland of Sand Point, situated north of Weston-super-Mare, is a mainly low water venue with broken ground at close range and offers all-year sport.*

Bigger tides fish best with 12 metre-plus springs favoured most. Fish two hours either side of low water.

SPECIES

Species include codling, dogfish, conger eel, bass, eel, plus an odd ray or sole. Winter gives a few big cod.

Summer offers the best conger fishing, along with bass, dogfish, eel, flatfish and the odd ray. September and October gives whiting and the odd sole. Codling can be caught from September to April.

BEST BAITS

Peeler crabs are best in summer, but ragworms will catch fish. Conger take whole squid. Lug and squid cocktails catch codling and whiting, although big baits are best for larger cod.

TACKLE

Use a single size 4/0 or 6/0 hook trace is the sensible option. Fish can be caught at around 80 yards, but distance can be an advantage. The tide is fairly strong here, so a 5oz-6oz grip lead is a must.

Conger eels can be quite large here, so it is advisable to take a gaff along with you.

GETTING THERE

Take the A371 off the M5 and head for Kewstoke. There is a small coastal road that runs along Sand Bay, finishing at a dead end with plenty of car parking space. It is about a 20-minute walk from here to the Point.

TACKLE SHOP

● *Chris' Angling Centre, 12 Regent St, Burnham, Tel: 01278 794442.*

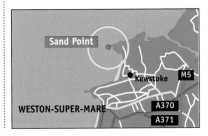

■ *This is a mark that can be fished from the comfort of your car. Knab Rock is just outside The Mumbles in Swansea Bay and is next to a good launch site for small boats.*

Shore anglers fish form the concrete esplanade, with three hours either side of high water best.

SPECIES

Autumn and winter are excellent seasons for large numbers of whiting and a few codling, along with dab and pouting. Spring and summer offer a wider range of species, including bass, dogfish, gurnard, strap conger, plaice, mackerel,

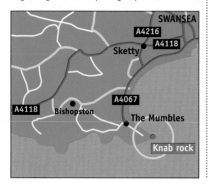

garfish and trigger fish. Big cod and bass are also caught here occasionally.

BEST BAITS

The best baits are lugworms or ragworms, strips of mackerel or peeler crabs.

TACKLE

This is mainly clean ground with a few snags, although a long cast might mean a snag on the boat moorings. Terminal rigs should be two or three-hook paternosters.

GETTING THERE

Follow the coast road from Swansea towards The Mumbles. Drive through the town and you will find Knab Rock on the left-hand side, just before the pier. Most people decide to fish adjacent to the launch site.

TACKLE SHOPS

● *Country Angling, 3a Church St, Gowerton, Tel: 01792 875050.*
● *Mainwarings Angling, 44 Vivian Rd, Sketty, Swansea, Tel: 01792 202245.*
● *Roger's Tackle, Sea Angling Centre, Pilot House Wharf, The Marina, Swansea, Tel: 01792 469999.*

■ *Llanmadoc, also widely referred to as 'The Tope Channel', is located on the North Gower coast towards the mouth of the Lougher Estuary.*

It is an open ground, sandy mark with a few rough patches giving access to a deepwater channel that, in its heyday when the channel used to be dredged, produced lots of tope to shore anglers. These days tope are occasionally caught by the few anglers who bother to fish for them, though it is the other species available that are more generally targeted.

SPECIES
Bass, flounder and dogfish are the three key species with ray, gurnard, dab, plaice, turbot, smoothhound, mackerel, mullet, whiting and codling also available at various times.

BEST BAITS
Fish with peeler crabs and live ragworms for bass, bunches of maddies for flounder and either mackerel, herring or frozen sandeels for dogfish.

TACKLE
Either a standard beach casting outfit or bass rod is ideal for general bottom fishing, with plenty of opportunity for lure fishing, especially around low water on the bigger tides.

GETTING THERE
Follow either the A4295 or A4271 to Llanrhidian, then head towards Llangennith. Turn right opposite the Greyhound pub and follow the lane through Landimore and Cheriton, passing the Beaufort pub. Follow the lane to its end, parking in a farm field behind the sand dunes. There is a £1.50 parking fee.

TACKLE SHOP
● *Country Angling, 3a Church St, Gowerton, Tel: 01792 875050.*

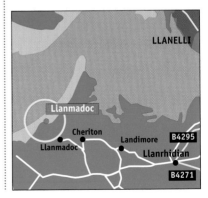

121

■ *The River Loughor, which flows into the Burry Estuary between Llanelli and Gorseinon, is noted by many anglers as one of the top flounder rivers in south-west Wales.*

The area has for many years hosted the famous Loughor Flounder Festival.

Most anglers start fishing at low water on small to mid-range tides, then fish right the way up to high water slack. Initially most fish will be concentrated in the main river channels, but as the water depth increases they spill out across the sand flats, and can often be caught with a few feet of the water line.

SPECIES
Between September and the New Year, large quantities of flounder are caught here, many of which are of a high average size. Silver eels, bass and mullet can be caught throughout the warmer months.

BEST BAITS
Best baits to use are peeler crabs, various types of marine worms and shellfish.

TACKLE
Standard beach gear will be adequate, but you will get more enjoyment using a lighter rod designed for catching flatfish. Present your bait on a flowing trace.

GETTING THERE
To get to the Loughor, exit the M4 at junction 47 and head towards Gorseinon. Access down to the river is possible at several locations near the railway and road bridges.

TACKLE SHOP
● *Country Stores, 3a Church St, Gowerton, Tel: 01792 875050.*

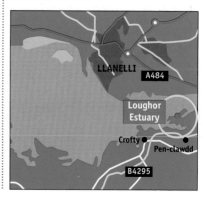

MONKNASH
South Wales

■ *This beach is a lovely expanse of sand fringed with rock outcrops to the west of Marcross. Monknash is not only popular with anglers because the western end is frequented by nudists in the summer.*

Fishing at low water on the larger tides produces the best results at this Bristol Channel venue, but your chances are improved at night.

SPECIES
The variety of fish is mixed and includes the chance of a big monkfish on a fish bait in summer. Run-of-the-mill fishing produces various ray, dogfish, turbot, bass, codling and smoothhound from the rockier areas.

This mark is noted for big thornback ray early in the season. Ray fishing is usually best after a

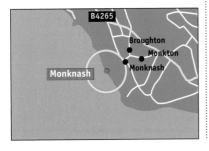

settled spell. You should beware of the flooding tide cutting off your retreat.

BEST BAITS
Top baits are fillets of fish, sandeel, squid and crab, but black lugworm and ragworm do catch.

TACKLE
Simple one-hook paternoster rigs are adequate for fishing over the relatively snag-free ground.

GETTING THERE
This is an awkward mark to find. Take the B4265 from Barry through Llantwit Major and then take the left turn for Marcross.

Turn right almost immediately for Monkton and Broughton. After these villages turn left for Monknash. Turn right and go through Monknash to the sea. You travel towards a farmhouse, but 20 yards before the farm, the road splits. Take the left road to the car park. Leave your vehicle, then walk down the hill and through the wood to the beach.

TACKLE SHOPS
● *Barry Angling Centre, 14 Park Crescent, Barry, Tel: 01446 747638.*
● *Ewenny Angling Supplies, 11b Ewenny Rd, Bridgend, Tel: 01656 662691.*

123

MONKSTONE POINT
South Wales

■ *Monkstone Point reaches into Carmarthen Bay between Tenby and Saundersfoot.*

The adjoining beach is best fished at night spent from low water up to two hours down. Dusk and dawn are the best times for bass. Spring and autumn are good for bass from the beach, while the summer is the time to fish the rocks.

Very strong undercurrents sweep around the headland and into the bays on the flood and ebb. Treat the area with caution.

SPECIES

Bass, ray, dab, plaice and flounder, dogfish and odd spurdog. There is always the chance of a tope. Mullet appear around the point during warm, settled spells in summer.

A rising tide on the main beach area is excellent for ray; try fishing in March and April, as the fish begin to move inshore to spawn. Plagues of whiting appear around October to April; mackerel strip is the best bait.

BEST BAITS

Razorfish and lugworms are the favourite baits. Fish strip takes ray, while cockles and lug tempt flatfish. Sandeels attract almost anything, particularly ray.

Cocktails are worth a try for most species. Peeler crabs cast close to the rocks at low water can produce bass. Baits for mullet can be bread crust or paste, harbour rag or even small pieces of king rag.

TACKLE

Use three-hook clipped or flapper rigs for flatfish

and whiting, single hook clipped down rigs for bass and spurdog, with a pulley Pennell for the ray. Tope require wire rigs on a running leger system.

Grip weights are essential, especially when the sea is rough. Use either a sliding float system for pollack, garfish, bass or mackerel. You could try lures for bass.

Hokkai-style rigs will catch fish. Try artificial eels cast out to sea or parallel to the beach. Mullet will take a bait fished under float.

GETTING THERE

Approach Saundersfoot on the M4, then go onto the A48 past Carmarthen towards St Clears along the A40. Go onto the A477 and head for the Begelly roundabout and take a sharp left towards the Fountain Head Inn. Take the left turn opposite the pub onto the B4316 into Saundersfoot.

Take your car onto the main Tenby to Saundersfoot road on the steep hill that leaves the village, passing the hotel at the top of the hill. Carry on through Broadfield. Turn off before you reach the junction of the A478 and head for Trevayne Farm. Park and it is a short walk down a steep path towards Monkstone.

TACKLE SHOPS

● *Anglers Corner, 1 Pill Rd, Milford Haven, Tel: 01646 698899.*
● *Milford Angling Supplies, The Old Custom House, The Docks, Milford Haven, Tel: 01646 692765.*

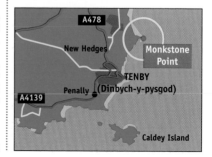

124

■ *Rhossili beach is what many anglers would term a classic bass surf beach. Running more or less due south and facing west, the beach consists of golden sand. When the wind is in the west, the surf can be impressive.*

Most anglers start fishing at low water until the few hours of the ebb. Night fishing is more productive than fishing in broad daylight.

SPECIES
Bass can be caught at Rhossili beach from March

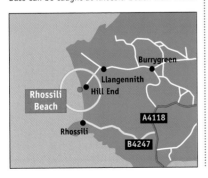

to November. Flounder show all year, but the best sport is in spring and autumn.

BEST BAITS
Lugworms are the best all-round bait, but razorfish can be a deadly.

TACKLE
The standard way to tackle the Gower's surf beaches is to fish during a steady surf using a basic single or two-hook paternoster rig. Use a standard beachcasting rod or specialist bass rod. Both can be matched with a 6500-sized multiplier reel or fixed-spool sea reel.

GETTING THERE
To get to Rhossili, follow the A4118 main south Gower road, from Swansea towards Upper Kilay. Then take the B4271 to Llanrhidian. Follow the signs for Burrygreen, then Llangennith. Access to the beach is via the caravan site at Hill End.

TACKLE SHOP
● *Country Angling, 3a Church St, Gowerton, Tel: 01792 875050.*

ST BRIDES
Newport, South Wales

■ *St Brides is the area of sea wall to the west of the mouth of the River Ebbw at Newport, starting at the old East Usk lighthouse and running for several miles.*

The sea wall, from which the vast majority of anglers fish, gives access onto mud flats which are covered at high tide. This mark is fishable from three hours before high water to about two hours after.

This is one of those venues which is fishable by anyone, and where long range casting is not always necessary. Indeed, during the summer the best fishing for the eel and flounder is often found by lobbing baits less than 30 yards into a few inches of water; fish as the flooding tide reaches the bottom of the sea wall. Night fishing can be more productive.

SPECIES
The major species here include silver eel and flounder with occasional bass, conger, sole and mullet throughout the summer, and whiting and cod throughout the autumn and winter.

BEST BAITS
Top baits for the summer species include small chunks of fresh peeler crabs, ragworms and lugworms. Small strips of fish are the best bait for the whiting, which have been plentiful in recent years.

Worms, crabs, squid and livebaits score well for the cod. Several double-figure cod are reported from St Brides, which is locally known at 'the lighthouse', each season.

TACKLE
For the smaller species, anglers use either two or three-hook paternoster rigs. Most anglers use a single hook or Pennell rig for cod, but wishbone rigs are another popular choice.

A 5oz breakout type lead will be needed if fishing at long range. It is better to use a plain flat lead at close range, allowing the tide to drag it slowly across the mud.

GETTING THERE
Follow the B4239 coast road from Newport towards Cardiff. The sea wall is reached from the Lighthouse pub car park, or at the end of Outfall Lane, a few miles down the road.

TACKLE SHOPS
● *Cwmbran Angling, 39 Richmond Road, Pontnewydd, Tel: 01633 868890.*
● *Pill Angling Centre, 160 Commercial Rd, Newport, Tel: 01633 267211.*
● *Sportsmail, 3 Allensbank Rd, Cardiff, Tel: 02920 343166. www.sportsmail.ltd.uk.*

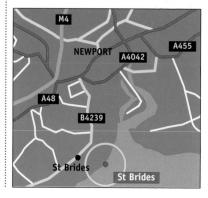

■ *This is a small tidal island just offshore at Sully. It is cut off from the mainland for about three hours either side of high water.*

The Monkey Pole and Green Island are the most popular hot spots. The first is an old Coastguard flag planted in a finger of rock on the eastern tip and is most productive. Green Island is an outcrop of rock on the western tip.

Sully Island is a low water venue, though a few anglers do fish over high water. Mid-range and spring tides between 13.5-15 metres on the Barry scale get results.

Anglers fishing this venue should be aware of the dangers of attempting to cross the 750 yard causeway when the tide has not fully receded or has started to flood. Many have tried and subsequently drowned when ignoring these dangers. Tide times are given on the notice board next to the causeway.

SPECIES
This is a top cod venue in autumn and winter, with a lot of double-figure fish reported each season. Other species include whiting, pouting and a few dogfish and flatfish.

The warmer months produce a lot of conger eels, including some good specimens, a few rays and increasingly good bass.

BEST BAITS
Black lugworms, ragworms, squid and crabs for the cod. Fish is the choice for the conger.

TACKLE
The area is swept by very strong tides, which coupled to the very rough sea bed demand grip leads of at least 5oz to hold bottom. Long casting is a distinct advantage here.

Popular rigs are the paternoster and pulley styles. Some sort of rotten-bottom rig to help minimise tackles losses is essential.

GETTING THERE
Follow the B4267 from Barry towards Cosmeston Lakes and Penarth and turn right into the beach road just past Sully village. Park in the car park at the end of the lane, near the pub, and buy a parking ticket.

TACKLE SHOP
● *Sportsmail, 3 Allensbank Rd, Cardiff, Tel: 02920 343166. www.sportsmail.ltd.uk.*

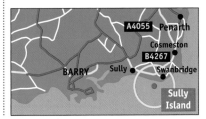

■ *This shallow storm beach on the tip of the Lleyn Peninsula produces bass from late April through to late November, but school bass are caught all year.*

At Aberdaron beach, your best chance of big bass or a ray is at low water in settling seas, after a storm on a spring tide.

SPECIES
Ray, mainly thornbacks, appear from late March and stay until mid-June, before reappearing in late September until early November. October and November offer whiting and coalfish, along with the odd codling.

Gullies running parallel with the beach hold bigger bass, small turbot and ray.

BEST BAITS
A peeler crab bait fished near the rough ground takes the better bass, but lugworms and ragworms also work. Mackerel strip or sandeels get ray, dogfish and bull huss. Try mussels, fish strip, squid, crabs, lug and rag.

TACKLE
Surf conditions usually tear up the sea bed, so powerful beachcasters, 15lb line and 5oz-6oz grip leads are needed. Calmer seas allow the use of bass rods, smaller reels and 12lb line for the dogfish, flatfish and bass.

Two or three-hook rigs tempt a bigger variety of species, but use a single-hook trace for bass and ray.

GETTING THERE
The B4413 from Caernarfon and Pwllheli ends in the village, where there is a car park on the right-hand side as you cross the bridge. Access to the beach is reached from this car park and is clearly signposted.

TACKLE SHOP
● *Adams Angling, 36 High St, Caernarfon, Tel: 01286 671300.*

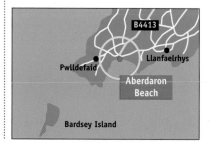

■ This is a beach where the list of species is not so great, but it makes up for it in the consistency of its fishing.

The sea bed has rock, boulders and occasional patches of cleaner ground, while the mid-beach area breaks up into coarse sand, gravel and shingle. A river flows on to the beach and this can destroy the fishing during times of heavy rain.

Moderate winds and a good surf are best for bass, but calm tides are favoured, but neaps over high water can give good bass and huss if you fish the rough and are willing to lose lots of tackle.

SPECIES
Bass dominate between April and June and again from August to October. Any huss tend to be caught in the May to August, with the same time seeing eel towards the river outflow.

September sees a fair run of whiting on the eastern end of Afon Wen beach. Dogfish, rockling and occasional flatfish make up the rest of the species.

BEST BAITS
Crabs or king ragworms take the bass, with fish/squid combinations best for huss, although it pulls in hordes of dogfish too. Worms and sandeels are ideal for winter whiting. Big baits of mussels single out large dab, which can move into the cleaner patches in late winter.

TACKLE
Your tackle losses can be heavy, so beachcasters, tough reels and 20lb line are favoured, but pick your spot carefully and you can get away with lighter bass tackle.

Stick to single-hook rigs or pulley rigs using a weak link to the lead when fishing the rough ground. The sand patches can be fished with normal two-hook rigs, but you will need grip leads to avoid tackle finding the snags.

Long casting is not needed because most fish come to casts of no more than 50 yards, though occasionally single bull huss are contacted at longer range.

Cast baits close to the lobster pot markers because they attract huss when freshly baited.

GETTING THERE
It is situated on the A497 between Porthmadog and Pwllheli and a mile east of Butlins. Look for a small unmarked white classified road, which brings you to a railway bridge. There is limited parking on both sides of the road. Now walk under the bridge and follow the rough track along to the beach.

TACKLE SHOPS
● *Adams Angling, 36 High St, Caernarfon, Tel: 01286 671300.*
● *D & E Hughes, 24 Penlan Street, Pwllheli, Tel: 01758 613291.*
● *Tywyn Bait & Tackle Centre, 1 Bryn-y-Mor, North Promenade, Tywyn, Tel: 01654 710046.*

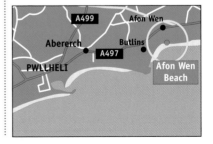

■ *Overlooked by Criccieth Castle, this mark lies on the west side of the town, and faces south-west in to Cardigan Bay.*

The beach is made up of rough ground and boulders, with patches of clean sand at long range. The sand is easily reached over low water, but over high water you're mostly casting into rough.

You can fish off the walkway at the top over high water, but in summer tourist activity limits it to a night-only venue. The far eastern end of the beach, near the rock headland, is backed by shingle and is easy to fish.

SPECIES
Bass, mackerel, dogfish, ray, dab and whiting.

BEST BAITS
Crab in the rough ground is best for the summer and autumn bass, or try spinning with artificial eels. Sandeels and mackerel take the ray, which show in April and May, and again in September and October. Dab and whiting appear in late September and go for worm tipped with a sandeel or piece of mackerel. Feathering during an evening high water in July and August takes good numbers of mackerel.

TACKLE
You need strong 5oz to 6oz beachcasters and 7000-sized reels loaded with 25lb line for fishing in to and over the boulders. A short cast finds the bass, but long casts are needed for the ray, dab and whiting to find the cleaner ground.

Best rig for bass is a pulley rig with a weak link system to the lead. The bass can be good size so stick to size 3/0 or 4/0 hooks. The pulley rig also works well for the ray. Switch to a two or three-hook rig for the dab and whiting, but use a lead lift to help the tackle skip over the snags.

GETTING THERE
Take the A497 from Porthmadog towards Criccieth. Entering the town, continue straight on, heading west. As you leave the town, there is a filling station on your left and then a left-turn posted Traeth (Beach). Turn onto this road and go down the hill. The car park is above the beach as the road goes back to the left at the bottom of the hill.

TACKLE SHOPS
● *D & E Hughes, 24 Penlan Street, Pwllheli, Tel: 01758 613291.*
● *Aber Discount Tackle, 3 Terrace Rd, Aberystwyth, Tel: 01970 611200*
● *Tywyn Bait & Tackle Centre, 1 Bryn-y-Mor, North Promenade, Tywyn, Tel: 01654 710046.*

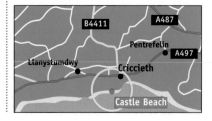

■ Dinas Dinlle is a sloping shingle beach on the open coast beyond the village of Llandwrog and has soft, clay cliffs on its seaward side.

A true storm beach, it is often exposed to the fury of westerly gales and ferocious surf. The shingle gives way to sand about 40 yards from the high tide line.

Night fishing for bass is popular because larger specimens are usually caught after dusk. The tide retreats a considerable distance during springs and bigger tides produce the best results.

The last three hours of the flood tide and first two of the ebb are the prime times and a 5oz grip lead is usually sufficient to hold bottom.

SPECIES

Dinas Dinlle beach is a good spot for bass and thornback ray. Other summer species include plaice, dab, bull huss and occasional turbot.

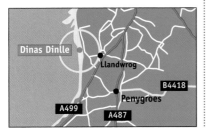

Mackerel appear during warm, calm periods.

Dogfish, codling, coalfish and whiting are caught during autumn and winter, although it should be avoided during April to September.

BAITS

Black lugworms are popular during winter and larger whiting are often hooked with mackerel-tipped baits. Large mackerel baits catch ray, dogfish, bull huss and bass, while in summer peeler crab is good for smaller species.

TACKLE

Some locals like to lob out large baits at low water as the tide begins to flood. Use standard beach gear. A three-hook rig using size 1 hooks will catch coalfish and whiting, while a few turbot may be caught using a single sandeel fished on a flowing trace and size 2/0 hook.

GETTING THERE

Dinas is clearly signposted from the main A499 to Pwllheli. The coast road runs behind the shingle bank.

TACKLE SHOPS

● *Adams Angling, 36 High St, Caernarfon, Tel: 01286 671300.*
● *D & E Hughes, 24 Penlan Street, Pwllheli, Tel: 01758 613291.*

■ *Porth Oer is also called 'Whistling Sands' because the coarse nature of the sand makes it squeak when walked on.*

This is a shelving beach flanked by a rocky headland to the left and cliff ground to the rear and right. A reef comes across at right angles from the headland, but only long-range casters reach it. There are other patches of rough ground scattered across the beach, but these can cover with sand during periods of calm weather.

The beach carries a big surf in south-west and west winds, but can be weedy after a blow.

SPECIES
Bass, codling, plaice, ray, gurnard, turbot, huss, wrasse, conger, dab, coalfish and whiting.

BEST BAITS
Sandeels take bass, turbot and the ray. Switch to lugworms for the winter flatfish and codling. Rag is a top plaice bait, especially tipped with a sliver of squid. A crab cast close to the rocks finds wrasse and bass. Mackerel strips at long range take gurnard, dogfish, conger and huss.

TACKLE
Use 5oz to 6oz beachcasters and 6500-sized reels with 15lb line for average conditions with no weed. After storms, go for a 7000-sized reel and 20lb to combat the weed and exposed snags. Top rigs are single-hook, clipped-down rigs with size 2/0 hooks for bass or 3/0 Pennell rigs for codling, huss and ray. Multi-hook rigs

with size 2 Aberdeens are best for the flatfish and whiting. A two-hook rig and size 1/0 hooks take big coalfish right in the surf tables.

The combined spring tide run and a big surf requires 6oz grip leads, but on average conditions a 5oz breakout lead is adequate.

GETTING THERE
From Bangor, take the A487 Caernarfon road, branching right on to the A499. Turn right at Llanhaelhearn on to the B4417 and head towards Tudweilog. After Tudweilog, Porth Oer is signposted. There is a car park at the top and access is down a steep road that leads directly on to the beach.

TACKLE SHOPS
● *Adams Angling, 36 High St, Caernarfon, Tel: 01286 671300.*
● *D & E Hughes, 24 Penlan Street, Pwllheli, Tel: 01758 613291.*

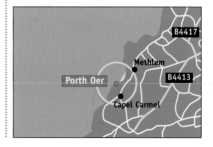

■ *A reliable beach throughout the year, it is often used for matches and a wide variety of species are caught. Being steeper shelving than most other local beaches, the south beach offers deep water at distance over clean sand with a few beds of shingle and weed.*

On this beach, night tides always produce more fish than daylight. The peak time for bass is September and October.

SPECIES
Codling, whiting, flounder and dab in winter, with bass, thornback ray, black bream, bull huss and dogfish during spring and summer.

BEST BAITS
Winter fishing requires lugworms or ragworms tipped with sandeel. White ragworm can be excellent at times. Thornback ray are taken on peeler crabs or fresh mackerel, but spotted ray like sandeels. Most bass fall either to lug, rag, peelers or sandeels.

TACKLE
At this mark, use two rods, one at distance and the other close in. Basic beach gear is all that is needed, with 5oz grip leads and flowing traces. Make sure that you use strong hooks when fishing for ray, because they can sometimes put quite a strain on your tackle. Big bass fall to spinners worked around the edge of Gimblet Rock over high water.

GETTING THERE
Pwllheli is reached on the A497 or A499. Follow the one-way system through to the centre of the town, then turn left (signposted Traeth beach) at the first roundabout. This goes to the mid-beach section with parking on the front. Alternatively, you can take the left-hand turn through the housing estate to the boatyards to fish the southern end.

TACKLE SHOPS
● **D & E Hughes, 24 Penlan Street, Pwllheli, Tel: 01758 613291.**
● **Tywyn Bait & Tackle Centre, 1 Bryn-y-Mor, North Promenade, Tywyn, Tel: 01654 710046.**

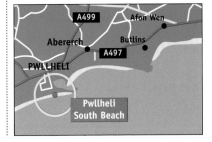

133

■ *This is a popular seafront mark in Colwyn Bay with fishing very close to your vehicle. The promenade is easy to see and is backed by a grassy bank.*

The best fishing is from September through to February. Fish from two hours before high water and over to two hours after from the railings, although this may vary with the height of the tide. Some anglers reckon that three hours before high and an hour after into darkness is best. Certainly your prospects will improve if there is a strong northerly wind.

SPECIES
Target fish include bass in late April to September, while plaice are caught from early April to September. Mackerel and herring feature in summer.

Winter in Colwyn Bay offers large numbers of whiting which arrive in late September and remain until February. Dogfish, small conger, codling and rockling are the main autumn and winter species. Codling are expected in November to February.

TACKLE
Tackle can be set up beside your vehicle. A standard beachcaster is ideal or this area. Two or three-hook rigs are best with 5oz grip leads. Size 1 and 2 hooks are suitable.

BAIT
Mackerel, lugworms, black lug, ragworms and sandeels are the main baits. Crabs are good, but not essential.

GETTING THERE
Turn off the A55 Queensferry to Colwyn Bay road, following the signs for Colwyn Bay promenade and Rhos-on-Sea. This brings you past the pier and along the main promenade.

TACKLE SHOP
● *Victoria Pier Angling Centre, The Promenade, Colwyn Bay, Tel: 01492 530663.*

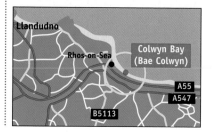

HOLYHEAD BREAKWATER
Anglesey

■ Holyhead breakwater extends in a dog leg into the Irish Sea and is split into two sections. The lower level allows access to the inner harbour, while there is an upper walkway on the outside wall. Fish three hours each side of high water, but fish can be caught throughout the tide, due to the tide receding from the wall's base over low water, and the problem of dragging fish across a stretch of rocks. Inner harbour catches are poor during summer, especially in daylight. This stretch tends to fish well only in winter after dark. The outer wall offers casting into rough ground, so tackle losses are high and rotten-bottom rigs are best. Distance casting is useful because the rough ground eases after 100 yards. Short casting into the rough can pay dividends. The breakwater end is used mainly for pleasure fishing. The ground is fairly clean, except for the left-hand corner.

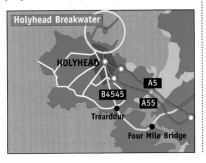

SPECIES
Main summer species from the outside wall are ballan wrasse, pollack and dogfish. Wrasse tend to be small and it can be difficult to catch fish above the local minimum size of 30cm.

Pollack weigh up to 3lb, but double-figure fish are possible, and dogfish go to 2lb. Other species at this mark include cuckoo and corkwing wrasse, rockling, ling, pouting, poor cod, codling, conger, whiting, tadpole fish and huss, to name just a few.

BEST BAITS
Top baits in summer are crabs and ragworms for wrasse, with sandeels and mackerel scoring for dogfish and pollack. Lugworms tempt whiting and dab from the inner harbour in winter.

GETTING THERE
Follow the A5 across Anglesey to Holyhead. In the town, follow the road towards the old ferry terminal alongside the railway line, turning left before the old terminal. Continue along this road and bear left towards the end for the breakwater. Parking is usually available along the full length of the roadway, but care must be taken not to cause obstruction to the maintenance traffic.

TACKLE SHOP
● *Anglesey Bait Centre, Gallows Point, Beaumaris, Tel: 01248 810009.*

135

■ *Located at the base of the Great Orme and facing out to the north is the Victorian pier at Llandudno. It has a platform at the end and surrounding railings, where safe angling is available, although there can be restrictions in storms. A parking area is located to the left of the pier, down a road leading to the Orme Drive.*

A daily tariff board is displayed on the side entrance to the pier. Fishing costs £1.25 a rod per day or £1.75 at night. Fishing is from 8am-4am at the end of the pier only. A ramp allows disabled access.

Llandudno is a very popular tourist spot, and parking can be a problem in summer, but is available close to the pier in winter.

SPECIES

Llandudno's summer species are bass, pollack, plaice, thornback ray, conger, scad, mullet, mackerel and wrasse. Codling, whiting, dab, coalfish, dogfish, conger and flounder are the winter regulars.

BEST BAITS

Use lug tipped with mussels or ragworms for codling and plaice. Crabs will catch the bass and wrasse, while fish baits should work well for the other species.

TACKLE

A standard beachcaster is ideal or this area. Use size 2/0 to 4/0 hooks fished on 18lb-20lb mainline. Float gear is good for mackerel, scad and mullet. The latter feed under the pier legs.

GETTING THERE

Take the A55 past Colwyn Bay towards Anglesey, but at Llandudno Junction turn onto the A470 to Llandudno and follow this road to the sea front.

TACKLE SHOP

● *Paddy's Bait & Tackle, adjacent to the Llandudno pier gate, Tel: 01492 877678.*

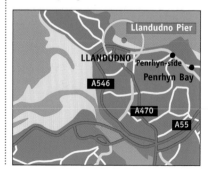

MOSTYN
North Wales

■ *Situated near Point of Ayr, this Dee estuary mark is one of the most easterly on the North Wales coast.*

The sloping banks are man-made and consist of broken boulders, giving way to mud and sand at low water. The current rips through the estuary over high water, so holding bottom can be impossible at times. The tide fishes at its best from two to three hours either side of low water.

SPECIES
You can expect to see dab from November to March, with eel and plaice in April and May. Good plaice can be caught as late as October. Whiting and codling show from October to February, with night best.

TACKLE
Use a powerful beachcaster to put your bait out on a sandbank, with 20lb mainline. Fish with two-hook paternoster rigs, carrying size 1 or 2/0 hooks. Terminal tackle losses can be high.

BAIT
Lugworms and mackerel are the essential winter baits, while peeler crabs and local rag work in summer. Lug catches all year. Feathers are best for mackerel.

GETTING THERE
Mostyn is on the A548 coast road near Coed Mawr and Point of Ayr. The banks are reached easily past the Coed Mawr market and over the railway bridge, which is visible from the main road that takes you to the beach.

TACKLE SHOP
● *Deeside Fishing Tackle, 28 Chester Rd East, Shotton, Tel: 01244 813674.*

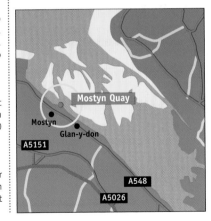

■ *Rhos Point is a popular bass mark at the site of an old pier, the remains of which can be seen in the sand.*

Bass anglers tend to fish three hours from low water on tides of 27ft and more. The bass are caught from July, but September and October are often the best times and fish can stay later. A stiff north-west wind creates the ideal conditions. Choose a rising tide around dawn or dusk.

SPECIES

Fishing from the beach produces bass, dogfish, whiting, and codling in winter, but there is a chance of plaice in September. A few strap conger may show.

East of Rhos Point is the marina and breakwater, where summer evenings produce mullet. The promenade and beach fishes at high water and one or two hours either side for bass, dogfish, whiting, codling and dab.

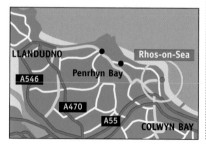

BEST BAITS

Use peeler crabs on a size 5/0 or 6/0 Aberdeen hook, but drop to a size 2/0 or 3/0 when using ragworms. Edible crabs are the top-rated bass bait, but king rag can be used, but may require a Pennell rig.

TACKLE

Spinning in the surf can be a good method, but casting out an edible crab bait is the most common tactic.

A two-hook rig or simple flowing trace with a single hook is best at Rhos Point. Use 25lb mainline ending in a three-way swivel. The hooklength running off the middle swivel should be 20in of 20lb line with a size 5/0 or 6/0 Aberdeen hook. The plain lead is attached to 20in of 15lb line on the bottom swivel. Long casts are unnecessary, with 50 metres ideal.

GETTING THERE

Turn off the A55 Queensferry to Conwy road and follow the signs marked for Colwyn Bay promenade and Rhos-on-Sea. Follow the promenade road along past the marina to the café at Rhos Point. Car parking here is ample and safe. From the car park, it is just a short walk to the beach.

TACKLE SHOP

● *The Tackle Box, 17 Greenfield Rd. Colwyn Bay, Tel: 01492 531104. Victoria Pier*

■ *When bad weather coincides with an early evening low water during November and December, then Talacre at the mouth of the River Dee is the place to fish for guaranteed sport.*

Some parts of this popular shoreline are quite shallow and suit distance casting, while others are deep with as much as 30 feet of water within lobbing range at low water.

Beware of the incoming tide at this mark, so that you don't get cut off.

SPECIES

Dab and whiting are the main species here on

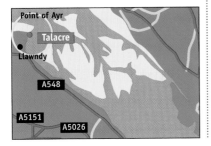

any tide at any time, but darkness and bigger tides give better and longer access to the main low-water channel. Other species include codling, flounder, plaice and bass.

TACKLE AND BAIT

A flowing trace or a two-boomed spreader or two-hook paternoster will catch plenty of fish. Small bomb leads will give plenty of movement, but you can use grip leads to anchor the bait. Baits fished just off the bottom on a dropper rig will catch whiting. Bottom baits pick up the dab.

GETTING THERE

Talacre village is near the Point of Ayr on the Welsh side of the Dee estuary. At the village, follow the right fork to a dead end at an embankment. Find a safe place to park the car and walk back to the embankment. Cross the embankment and cut across the shore to the green light. It's best to travel light!

TACKLE SHOP

● *Deeside Fishing Tackle, 28 Chester Rd East, Shotton, Tel: 01244 813674.*

139

■ *This beach is a popular venue on the Dee estuary, which runs between Wirral and North Wales. The estuary is wide and shallow, with a tide that races in across the flat sands, so make sure that you keep an eye on a rising tide and do not take any chances.*

The best fishing is an hour-and-a-half either side of low water, but flounder can be caught all the way through to the top of the tide, even for the first hour of the ebb.

SPECIES

The first run of flounder enter the Dee estuary at the end of March or the beginning of April. They come in after spawning and can provide hectic sport with bags of 20 fish providing really excellent fishing.

During summer there's also a good chance of catching school bass, with bigger fish showing every now and again. Whiting and codling are taken in winter.

BEST BAITS

Use pieces of peeler crab or ragworms for flounder. Lug and crab produces cod, but whiting like lug tipped with mackerel.

TACKLE

Using a lightweight 12 or 13ft beachcaster and tripod is best here, with either a multiplier or fixed-spool reel. Snags are rare so it is possible to get away with 15lb line, plus a shockleader. Use size 1 and 2 hooks. Grip leads of 5oz are the best average, but anglers with room for manoeuvre can work the beach with a rolling lead. Many anglers make the mistake of casting well over the fish. Yet they can be caught under the rod tip in inches of water.

This is also a venue for a haversack, rather than a heavy tackle box, because once the tide starts to flood, anglers are kept on the move. Look for a good tide with a steady breeze to whip up a small surf.

GETTING THERE

Access along the Wirral peninsula is easiest via the A540, either from Chester or Liverpool. At Caldy, take the B5141 and turn left into Shore Lane. Follow this towards Caldy Golf Club and use the public car park on the right. From here, it is an easy walk to the beach.

TACKLE SHOP

● *Parke's Angling, Birkenhead, Tel: 0151 652 0606.*

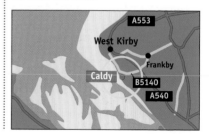

■ *Otterspool promenade is one of the most consistent marks on the River Mersey.*

Avoid the biggest tides because the sheer volume of water makes fishing uncomfortable. The river dries out, so plan a session for three hours before and up to two hours after high water.

SPECIES

Fishing at Otterspool starts in late April with flatfish and the first of the eel and improves steadily as the weather gets warmer, until the first whiting appear in autumn, followed by codling in October. The June to September period is best for eel and dab, then whiting arrive and stay until February, while codling to 5lb start showing in October and can still be around in late January.

BEST BAITS

Crabs are absolutely essential when eel fishing as they rarely show an interest in any other bait. The prime baits for whiting and codling are black lug tipped with mackerel or mussels. Crabs always work.

TACKLE

All of the species come within a short casting distance, but some days when a longer cast will produce a few extra whiting.

Grip leads up to 6oz are essential to combat the strong flowing tide, although a rolling weight can catch a few extra fish sometimes.

GETTING THERE

Take the A5036 from Liverpool's city centre towards the airport. The road runs parallel with the Mersey. After about three miles it becomes Riverside Drive, Otterspool. There are places along here where it is possible to park and fish alongside your car.

TACKLE SHOP

● *Champs Tackle, Unit 35, Garston Industrial Estate, Garston, Tel: 0151 494 3029.*

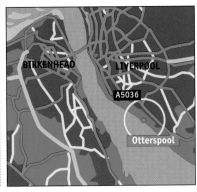

■ This beach is on the east side of Perch Rock, New Brighton, is an outstanding spot for low-water fishing on the River Mersey. Perch Rock itself is a waste of time at high water, as the tide is too strong.

Fishing about two hours either side of low water is best, though ideally, you should be fishing in darkness.

SPECIES
The beach has a year-round character, starting in mid-April when flounder push up into the deep-water gutter, followed soon afterwards by good-sized plaice. School bass also show in summer.

The beach is at its busiest from the end of September when the first of the whiting arrive. Codling arrive in October. Both species, along with the dab, stay right through to February before they disappear again.

BEST BAITS
Peeler crabs are essential in summer, though ragworms and lugworms do catch fish. The latter are likely to be attacked by crabs. Winter sport is more dependent on black lug tipped with a tiny piece of mackerel, mussel or crab.

TACKLE
A 12ft or 13ft standard beachcaster will do nicely for this mark. You should fit it with either a multiplier or fixed-spool reel, carrying about 18lb mainline. A 60lb shockleader is advisable. Grip leads of 5-6oz work best and hooks should be about size 1 or 2.

GETTING THERE
Take the M53 Wirral motorway or approach via Liverpool using the Kingsway Mersey Tunnel. Follow the signs for New Brighton and on to King's Parade (A554).

Fort Perch Rock is clearly visible before reaching New Brighton and you should turn left off the main road towards the fort. There is a free car park and only a short walk to the beach.

TACKLE SHOP
● *Ken Watson Tackle, Wallasey, Merseyside, Tel: 0151 6384505.*

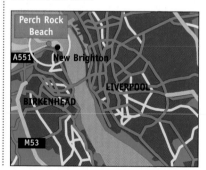

■ The Red Rocks mark lies at the end of the Wirral peninsula, which separates the Dee and Mersey, as they flow into the Irish Sea. Red Rocks are outcrops of sandstone on the beach near the town of Hoylake.

Shore anglers get great spring fishing here, but they do have to keep a wary eye on the flood tide rushing across the Wirral sands. It is a long walk for the best fishing, because the action starts at low water. However, the incoming tide moves fast and it is essential to travel light, while keeping a careful lookout to avoid being stranded.

If you fish at Red Rocks, avoid tides of 28ft and more because the fast-moving tide can be risky. Start fishing an hour after low water and work back to the high water mark.

SPECIES
This is a popular mark for flounder from April onwards. Although a few bass add interest. During May, when fishing reaches a peak, the sea beds teems with fish.

BEST BAITS
Ragworms are the best bait in April when there are few peeler crabs about. Once local crabs appear, the fish go mad for crab baits.

TACKLE
Two-hook paternoster rigs are popular, while your reel should carry an 18lb mainline and 50lb shockleader to allow for a 5oz lead. The hook

traces are 18in long and made from 18lb line and placed 12in and 30in from the lead. The top hooklength is 12in-18in long and is at least 20in above the lower one.

Fish are further out early in the tide, so longer casts are needed at this time. Once they swim in the deeper channels, they can be under your rod tip.

Light tackle, such as a 3oz lead, makes a change from normal beach fishing.

GETTING THERE
Hoylake is at the western corner of the Wirral. Follow the A540 from Chester.

TACKLE SHOP
● *John's Bait & Tackle, Wallasey, Tel: 0151 6391069.*

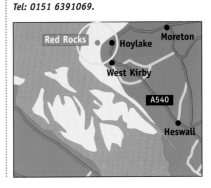

SEAFORTH ROCKS
Merseyside

■ *This is one of the River Mersey's top shore marks and is located near the river mouth, at the Liverpool dock estate.*

Cod are the main target at Seaforth Rocks, with evening and night sessions best, particularly either side of high water.

The rocks dominating the venue were used to create a huge deepwater harbour for container ships, but provide a casting platform into a deep channel. Angling is banned inside the docks. Avoid the biggest tides because of the powerful currents, and beware of the large gaps between the slippery rocks.

You do need a permit to fish the Seaforth docks. These are issued by the North West Association of Sea Angling Clubs. Ask for details at local tackle shops.

SPECIES
Winter fishing at Seaforth Rocks is headed by cod, whiting and dab. Dab can be caught all year, but the main season begins with the arrival of whiting in October. Codling usually appear in the middle of November, while larger fish take baits in December.

Dense shoals of whiting can provide hectic sport, especially during early evening as the light fades.

BEST BAITS
Use lug tipped with a piece of mackerel for whiting. Black lug or crabs take the cod.

TACKLE
Use a standard beachcaster with a 7000-size reel to cope with the rough snags. Mainline should be 20lb with a suitable shockleader.

A large helping of black lug should be fished on a Pennell rig carrying size 4/0 or 3/0 hooks. Use strong patterns, such as Mustad Uptide Viking. Some anglers use a pulley rig for cod.

Grip leads are essential with 6oz best. The deep channel runs fairly close, but a longer cast of 80 metres will put your bait on a mussel bed. Long casts do not necessarily produce more bites.

GETTING THERE
Follow the M57 and turn onto the A59. Take the A5036 (Regents Road) where you find the terminal entrance.

TACKLE SHOP
● *Anfield Tackle, 119 Oakfield Rd, Liverpool, Tel: 0151 260 8223.*

SPECIES
Dab, flounder, plaice, eel, whiting and codling.

BET BAITS
Most baits work, but peeler crab is good. Lugworms will take dab and codling, while mackerel strip gets whiting.

TACKLE
Use a standard beachcaster and reel loaded with 15lb mainline. Two-hook paternoster rigs with 20lb hook snoods and Aberdeen hooks in size 1 and 2 take flatfish, eel and whiting. Use a size 2/0 hook for codling. Aim to cast about 100 yards into the main channel to be effective. A 5oz lead may be needed in order to combat the strong tide, but a plain weight allows your bait to move on the bottom.

GETTING THERE
Take the M53 into Seacombe and then the A554 to New Brighton. The A554 runs parallel to the promenade. Turn right into King Lake Road and head towards the promenade. There is plenty of parking on the roads, but vehicles are not allowed on the promenade.

TACKLE SHOP
● *John's Bait & Tackle, 75-77 Poulton Rd, Wallasey, Tel: 0151 639 1069.*

■ *Dab are an all-year feature of this popular mark on the Wirral side of the River Mersey. Vale Park is at the western end of a promenade running from Seacombe to New Brighton.*

On an ebbing tide, a big bank of sand at Vale Park pushes the water away from the Egremont promenade wall and creates an eddy for about two hours. The swirling eddy is usually packed with fish.

There are also some flounder, plaice and eel during summer. In winter the dab are joined by whiting and codling. The best fishing is on 29ft-30ft tides. Best times are two hours before low water and two hours of the flood.

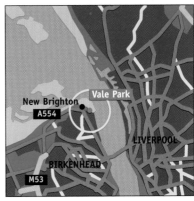

145

■ *This long, shallow beach comes alive in winter when anglers seek whiting and codling.*

Cleveleys is at the centre of an eight-mile stretch of Fylde Coast beaches running from Blackpool North Shore through to Fleetwood. The A584 runs alongside the beach and anglers can stop and begin fishing almost anywhere.

SPECIES
The main winter fish are codling and whiting, though dab and rockling also show. Dogfish show in milder weather. Bass are caught in late summer, particularly at a dusk low water. Small turbot, coalfish, whiting, dab and plaice can show, but as extras.

BEST BAITS
Crabs are best, but have a selection of lugworms, black lug, ragworms and white rag. Fish baits are good for whiting.

TACKLE
Standard beach gear or light bass rods are suitable for most of the year at Cleveleys, with sturdier rods only required during the winter when big fish may be about. Grip leads of 5oz cope with most conditions. Moving baits on size 1 hooks are successful in summer, but in winter use size 4/0 Pennell rigs with larger baits, anchored with a 6oz lead.

GETTING THERE
The easiest route is to enter Blackpool on the M55 from the M6. Follow the signs for the airport until you reach the promenade. Turn right at Squire's Gate, past three piers and onto Cleveleys. Car parking is plentiful.

TACKLE SHOP
Chris Webb Bait & Tackle, 52a St Anne's Rd, Blackpool, Tel: 01253 470004.

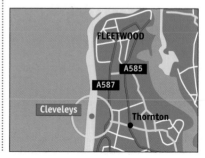

■ *This mark is located on the Ribble estuary and offers good fishing for flounder from March to the end of July.*

Average tides fish best, with fishing close in with light tackle over slack tide to low water producing good sport.

Further east, there are the shrimpers and boats, where fishing in between produces good sport for flounder and eel. Keep an eye on the tide coming in on the River Ribble.

Close by is Fairhaven, where the best fishing is opposite the lake for bags of flounder, eel and mullet. Average tides fish best, but a tide above 28ft reveals a retaining wall.

SPECIES
Expect good bags of flounder, eel and mullet.

BEST BAITS
Top baits are ragworms, shrimps or peeler crabs.

TACKLE
Use a standard beach rod with either a multiplier or fixed-spool reel loaded with 15lb mainline.

Float fishing with light tackle can be good fun for eel and flounder.

GETTING THERE
Lytham is situated on the A584 from Preston. Walking out onto the wall can be a messy job, and it is best to stay on top of the bank until you see the wall coming back onto the mud. Tread very carefully because there is some quicksand in this area.

TACKLE SHOP
Chris Webb Bait & Tackle, 52a St Anne's Rd, Blackpool, Tel: 01253 470004.

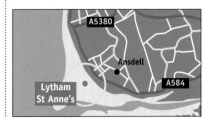

■ Marine beach is a noted mark for plaice, flounder and early bass. The locals often fish over high water as the tide builds up in front of Marine Hall and westwards for about 100 yards.

The Dronsfield Road area, about half-a-mile to the west, has deeper water and a stronger tidal flow, which can produce large bass, eel, plaice and codling.

Similar catches are made from the Fleetwood

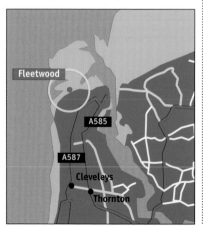

Channel at the mussel beds to the lifeboat station. Smaller tides are best here.

SPECIES
It is not unknown for codling to show in July and August. Most success will be for flounder and eel as they move into the river section in March and April. Bass and plaice are also caught.

BEST BAITS
Harbour rag and rag work well, but crabs are usually best.

TACKLE
Casts of 100 yards or more on a flowing trace will catch plaice, while an 18in-24in clipped-down hooklength lands bass and flounder. Use a grip lead and, as the tide becomes stronger, you can reduce your casting distance accordingly, otherwise weed will be a problem.

GETTING THERE
Follow the A587 or A585 into Fleetwood and the mark is located on the sea front road.

TACKLE SHOP
● *Chris Webb Bait & Tackle, 52a St Anne's Rd, Blackpool, Tel: 01253 470004.*

148

MORECAMBE
Lancashire

■ Although not on an estuary, Morecambe is similar to an estuary venue, because banks dry at low tide leaving channels and there are mussel beds, boulders and sand.

The promenade has a flounder, bass and eel mix, but winter produces whiting and codling. Free permits for the North Wall are available at local tackle shops.

The nearby Heysham power station attracts plenty of school bass to the area. Bigger fish do show, usually in the early morning at low water over the boulders.

SPECIES

Flounder and eel dominate, but plaice and bass are possible. Winter species are whiting, codling and flounder.

BEST BAITS

Top baits are peeler crabs and ragworms. Try small lures or big baits for the bass.

TACKLE

You will need a rod capable of casting 4oz-6oz leads, due to the need to cast good distances over the patchy ground and in strong tides.

Fish with simple one, two or three-hook paternoster rigs using size 1/0 to 3/0 hooks.

GETTING THERE

From M6 northbound towards Lancaster, take the A589 towards Morecambe. Turn left onto the B5273, which terminates at a T-junction between Morecambe and Heysham. Choose a spot on the promenade between Sandilands and the Battery Hotel.

TACKLE SHOP

● *Gerry's of Morecambe, 5-7 Parliament St, Morecambe, Tel: 01524 422146.*

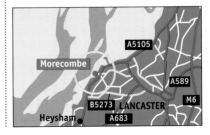

■ Rossall Point is a noted all-year mark on the Fylde coast, which is best from September to March. The Point is at the northern end of the beach, which is covered with gullies, rocky outcrops and groynes. Average tides of 26-29 feet are usually best.

The Rossall Coastguard lookout tower is a noted reference point, while locals consider the best fishing is on the Coastguard side of groyne 53. Try fishing over low water opposite the hospital or 500 yards north at The Plaque, both of which have rough ground.

Most of the rough ground is found over low water, but don't get trapped by the water running behind you on spring tides. Best times here are one-and-a-half hours either side of low water, or three hours up and one-and-a-half to two hours down. Night tides are best.

SPECIES

Codling and whiting show at Rossall Point from late summer, with larger fish expected in autumn and winter. Large flounder, eel and bass are caught in June and July.

BEST BAITS

Worms and crabs are best for codling. White rag is a good bait for whiting. Cocktail baits are popular; try lug and rag, crab and razorfish or lug and white rag.

TACKLE

Fish with standard beach gear and clipped-down rigs for 60-100 yards casts. You will need leads from 3oz to 6oz.

Use Pennell rigs clipped down or a size 2/0 single hook clipped down for 100-yard casting or bigger baits.

A two-hook paternoster is ideal for short-range work, using size 1 or 2 Aberdeen hooks. You could try a Wishbone rig at low water for better casting. Crab baits can be mounted on size 2 or 1/0 hooks.

GETTING THERE

Rossall Point is on the northwest side of Fleetwood. Follow the A587 or A585 into town and the mark is on the seafront.

TACKLE SHOP

● *Chris Webb Bait & Tackle, 52a St Anne's Rd, Blackpool, Tel: 01253 470004.*

■ *Flounder sport on the River Wyre peaks in spring, but does offer good fishing from March to October. Fish two hours up to high water from the mud. Remember that once the tide comes in you will have to move back on to the grass. You can fish for eel at high tide, into the boulders that show at low tide.*

SPECIES
At Stanah, flounder are the main target from spring to autumn, but you can catch plaice, eel and mullet as well. Peak flounder time is the end of May and early June.

BEST BAITS
Flounder like harbour ragworms (known locally as 'creeper') or lugworms tipped with harbour rag. Peeler crabs are the best bait for both flounder and eel.

TACKLE
At this mark, short casting between 15 and 25 yards is all that is required, certainly no more than 50 yards. You should use a standard beach rod, capable of casting a 6oz lead, and attach a suitable reel.

A moving lead should be used when the tide slackens; try a plain weight or removed several grips wires. Use one, two or three-hook paternoster rigs, although a one-up, one-down rig can be successful.

GETTING THERE
At junction 32 on the M6 take the M55 and then at junction 3, take the A585 to Poulton-le-Fylde. Follow the signs to Thornton and Stanah. There is a car park on the bank and it is a short walk to the favoured pylons area

TACKLE SHOP
● *Chris Webb Bait & Tackle, 52a St Anne's Rd, Blackpool, Tel: 01253 470004.*

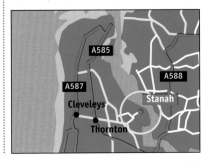

■ *This mark is a shallow, sandy beach with boulders, where sport generally starts with the first peel of crabs in late April or early May and ends in September.*

Rough sea conditions are best for bass in daylight when weed can be a problem. Flounder fishing over shallow ground is best from three hours before high water. Both species are caught close in at low water.

The tide ebbs for about one mile, so care should be taken when fishing a flooding tide because it races in at almost walking speed.

SPECIES
Bass, flounder, eel and occasional codling.

BEST BAITS
Peeler crabs for flounder. Large baits, consisting of lugworms and ragworms, for bass.

TACKLE
Use a light bass rod and a multiplier reel loaded with 15lb line. Grip leads are needed when the tide is flooding over shallow ground. Use two or three-hook traces for flounder and school bass, or a single hook with a large bait for bigger fish. Keep gear to a minimum by carrying bait and tackle in a shoulder bag. This will allow you to move about easily.

GETTING THERE
Take the A595 and A596 from Carlisle to Wigton, then turn onto the B5302 for Silloth. Beckfoot is three miles south of Silloth, on the B5300. Alternatively, you can follow the B5300 north from Maryport.

TACKLE SHOP
● *Graham's Guns & Tackle, 9-15 South William St, Workington, Tel: 01900 605093.*

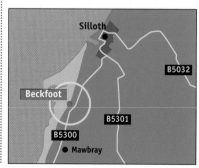

DUBMILL POINT
Cumbria

■ *Located near Mawbray is Dubmill Point, a top bass mark which is relatively unknown, outside of the North West.*

The coast between Beckfoot to Mawbray is noted for bass and double-figure fish are caught each year. Although bass are caught around the village of Mawbray, it is Dubmill Point that is the favoured mark.

Mawbray is fished only at high water with spring tides better than the neaps. A lively sea produces the best results. Beckfoot, which requires a 30-minute walk, is fished over low water. Don't get cut off by the incoming tide.

SPECIES
July marks the start of the better bass fishing and this continues into October, with night fishing best. Other species are flounder and eel.

BEST BAITS
Lugworms and ragworms can catch as many fish as peeler crabs.

TACKLE
A bass rod or beachcaster can be used here, with big hooks and big baits the key. Long casts are

not necessary, but there can be a strong tide so use a grip lead.

GETTING THERE
Dubmill Point is near Mawbray, which is reached on the B5300 coast road from either Silloth to the north or Maryport to the south.

TACKLE SHOP
● *Rod & Line, 19 High Street, Wigton, Tel: 016973 45744.*

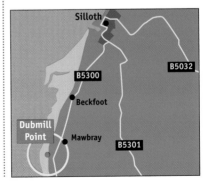

153

■ *This area used to be a commercial port, but times have changed and it is now used as a leisure boating marina.*

The two long arms to the harbour have a reputation with local anglers for providing them with some superb action throughout the year. The last 100 yards of the wall is where the cod are caught. There are numerous mussel beds which attract plaice.

SPECIES
Big plaice and codling are the two main species and at times the sport can be hectic.

Flounder and eel are present in force during the summer. From mid-September through to November, codling in the 1lb-3lb range are caught, with bags of 10 or more possible.

BEST BAITS
Peeler crabs are best for the flounder and eel. Plaice and codling prefer lugworms, or lug and squid cocktails.

TACKLE
Some of the ground fished here is very rough, so your line needs to be at least 20lb breaking strain. There is also a strong tidal run, which calls for lead weights of 5oz and above.

GETTING THERE
Take the M6 to Penrith and leave it at junction 40 for the A66 to Workington. Join the A5086 just after Cockermouth and then take the A594 to Maryport.

TACKLE SHOPS
● *Graham's Guns & Tackle, 9-15 South William St, Workington, Tel: 01900 605093.*

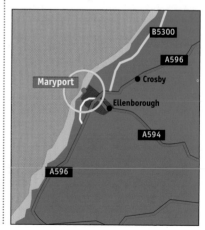

NETHERTOWN
Cumbria

■ *Nethertown is a winter venue for codling, whiting and occasional conger in a mixture of weed-covered rocks and sand patches. It fishes equally well at low water and from the steep shingle high water mark.*

A south-westerly wind in darkness gives the best conditions with two hours either side of low and high water the prime time. Find where the shingle bottom meets the stones and cast there at high water to locate codling.

SPECIES
Codling up to 6lb, with occasional better fish, show from September through to February. Whiting make an appearance from November.

BEST BAITS
Peeler crabs, lugworms and ragworms all fish well at this mark. Worms tipped with mackerel take bigger whiting.

TACKLE
The rocky ground requires heavy line and simple, one-hook traces. Tackle losses can be kept down by using breakout leads. Lighter line with two-hook, clipped-down rigs can be used on the sand. Weed on the line can be a serious problem over high water.

GETTING THERE
Turn off the A595 at the southern end of Egremont towards Middletown and follow the signs for Nethertown village. Cross the railway bridge and go on to the shore car park.

TACKLE SHOPS
● *The Compleat Angler, 4 King St, Whitehaven, Tel: 01946 695322.*
● *The Tackle Shack, George St, Whitehaven, Tel: 01946 693233 or 590714.*

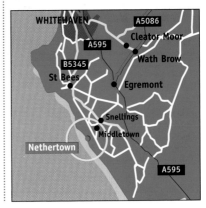

155

SILLOTH
Cumbria

■ Silloth is one of the most notable flounder marks in Cumbria. It lies on the Solway Firth just west of Carlisle.

There are a number of good marks here, especially at the extreme north and south ends. Look out for a trellis light on the promenade south of Silloth. It's called Cote Light and can give big catches.

Flounder start to make an appearance around mid-April, but it is not until late May when they are found in their thousands. Action peaks around June, but by mid-July the sport starts to slow down. August is fairly slow and by September it is really not worth fishing the mark.

Low water and the first part of the flood are considered the most hectic hours. High water is unproductive, even when low water is fishing well.

SPECIES

Flounder are the main target. Other species regularly encountered are mullet, bass, plaice, eel, a few dab and the odd sea trout.

BEST BAITS

The flounder sport coincides with the peeler crab season, which is the main reason for the fish coming to this mark in such large quantities. Worm baits do catch the odd fish, but the hard-back crab strip your hook within seconds of it hitting the sea bed.

Peeler crabs can be collected from around the breakwaters and under rocks throughout the months of May, June and July.

TACKLE

A simple beach outfit is all that is required to fish Silloth. One or two-hook traces made with size 1 or 1/0 hooks will do the job for the flounder and eel, but a slightly heavier set up may be required when targeting bass.

You could try using a baited spinner for the mullet and sea trout, but patience is the key to success when using this method.

GETTING THERE

From the south, it is best to turn off the M6 at junction 41 on to the B5305 through Wigton. Once there take the B5302 to Silloth. If approaching from the north, take the A595 to Wigton and then take the B5302 to Silloth.

TACKLE SHOP
● J B Blake's, 6 Crissel St, Silloth,
Tel: 01697 331245.

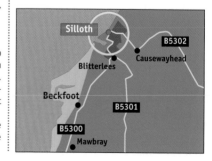

156

WHITEHAVEN PIERS
Cumbria

■ *There are two piers at Whitehaven – the west and the north – and both produce good catches throughout the year.*

The north pier is the easier of the two when it comes to access and fish-ability, but the west pier tends to produce the better results. The beaches either side of the two piers are extremely productive as well, so if the piers are too crowded you can fish these instead.

The best time to fish is two hours before and two hours after high water.

SPECIES
There are usually codling and whiting at this mark throughout the winter. Summer sees the start of the mackerel sport, which can be quite hectic on the right tides.

There have been cod to 35lb caught in the past, but most anglers get codling in the 2lb-6lb bracket, that is if you can get through the whiting. Other species include pollack, coalfish, rockling, dab, flounder and mullet.

BEST BAITS
Lugworms are the only choice when it comes to winter sport at Whitehaven piers. Fresh mackerel strip is the best bait for pollack, coalfish, mullet and mackerel. Mackerel head and guts or lugworm will take bass. Black lug will take flounder, dab and rockling. Try tipping your baits with squid for the cod.

TACKLE
Paternoster rigs with size 3/0 to 5/0 hooks are best for cod, but a simple three-hook rig using size 1/0 hooks will help you bag up on whiting. You can spin or float fish with fish strip for mackerel during summer, and you are likely to pick up coalfish, pollack and mullet as well. Bottom fishing in summer produces flounder, dab, rockling and the odd bass.

GETTING THERE
If you are coming in from the north, then you need to follow the A596. If you are coming from the south, take the A595. Both roads will take you into the town where the seafront and piers are signposted.

TACKLE SHOPS
● *The Compleat Angler, 4 King St, Whitehaven, Tel: 01946 695322.*
● *The Tackle Shack, George St, Whitehaven, Tel: 01946 693233 or 590714.*

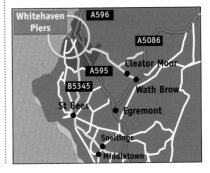

■ *Gansey is an excellent venue at the south of the island that fishes well all year, but really comes into its own for good bags of dogfish and coalies during the dark evenings of autumn and winter. It is a flat, sandy beach with a rough ground at the low water mark. This is the most popular time for competitions, as the tide races in on the flood for a couple of hours.*

Fishing over high water can be very productive for coalies and the odd flounder, with short casting all that is needed, but pick a small tide.

SPECIES
Dogfish, coalfish and flounder.

BEST BAITS
Sandeels and mackerel are the top baits, but peelers and lugworms tempt the coalies.

TACKLE
Stick with simple two-hook rigs. Although the bottom is rough at low water, there is no need for a rotten-bottom attachment. A gentle lob finds the fish, so any beachcaster set up will do. As the tide floods a longer cast is needed to reach the weed, but at high water it is back to shore casts.

GETTING THERE
Take the A5 from Douglas and head South. Gansey is the beach half a mile away from Port St Mary. Park by the Shore hotel where there is a slip down to the beach.

TACKLE SHOP
● *Tackle Box Too, Strand Road, Port Erin, Tel: 01624 836343.*

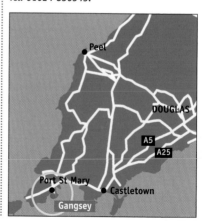

■ *Almost any species can turn up around this first-class rock mark. Situated on the south-east coast of the island, Langness has a terrific tide race. The area around the lighthouse has some of the best fishing. It is generally regarded as a low water mark because most of the best rocks are covered at high water.*

SPECIES
Dogfish, bull huss, ballan and cuckoo wrasse, pollack, mackerel, dogfish, conger and gurnard.

BEST BAITS
Live or artificial sandeels, squid, lugworms, ragworms, crabs and mackerel.

TACKLE
A two-hook, clipped-down trace is used to fish the bottom. Fish down the side of the rocks for wrasse with a single hook rig.

Pollack are taken by spinning sandeel or artificial eel, with mackerel and launce also falling to this method. Mackerel or squid fished on a running leger are used to tempt the many congers that frequent the various gullies.

GETTING THERE
From Douglas, head towards Castletown, going past the airport. Take the left turn at the roundabout and head towards Derbyhaven. Turn right at the cottages and make your way towards the golf club. Take the track on the right, which goes across the course, and keep going until you get to the car park. The lighthouse is on the right, but there is also good fishing to the left.

TACKLE SHOP
● *Tackle Box Too, Strand Road, Port Erin, Tel: 01624 836343.*

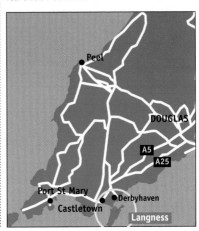

159

■ *Manx Match is the top match venue on the Isle of Man, especially between May and October when up to 40 dogfish are often required to win a four-hour competition.*

Events are held over low water to avoid the strong tides that sweep around the Point of Ayre. During May and June there are also bonus bull huss, which reach double figures, and there is always a few pollack, coalfish and odd codling.

SPECIES
Dogfish, bull huss, pollack, coalfish and codling.

BEST BAITS
Sandeels and mackerel.

TACKLE
Distance is not always necessary, but a 12ft-13ft beachcaster is are a must. The ground is snaggy in places, so a Daiwa SL20SH or similar reel is an advantage. A three-hook clipped-down trace armed with three small sandeels is best for dogfish, but mackerel can be effective on occasions. Bull huss often feed on the turn of the tide.

GETTING THERE
Take the A10 coast road from Ramsey to Bride

and turn right at the roundabout by the church. Now follow the A16 and head for the Point of Ayre. When you reach the landfill tip, the track down to the car park is at the edge of the venue.

TACKLE SHOP
● *The Ramsey Warehouse, 37 Parliament St, Ramsey, Tel: 01624 813092.*

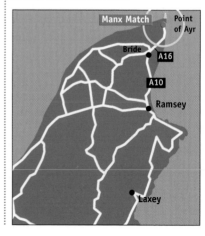

■ *Point West is a first-class venue for match and pleasure anglers and just about any species can turn up here.*

A strong tide race means that the venue can be comfortably fished for only two hours either side of high water on a small tide.

SPECIES

Coalfish, dogfish, tope, gurnard, dab, plaice, pollack, mackerel and codling.

BEST BAITS

The usual selection of fish and worm baits take fish at this mark, but sandeels and mackerel account for most.

TACKLE

A 12ft-13ft beachcaster with any decent reel copes with most situations as the ground is relatively clean. Rigs vary from one hook to three-hook paternosters, depending on the type of day.

A flat calm sunny day sometimes requires a little more distance to get among the dogfish regularly, but otherwise the fish tend to feed close in. When fishing further to the south of the venue, there is a good chance of tope during the summer, so have some wire traces.

Grip leads are a must at Point West, but there is no need to go any higher than 6oz when fishing over high water.

GETTING THERE

Take the A10 coast road from Ramsay to Bride, and turn right at the roundabout by the church. Follow the A16 for the Point of Ayre, driving past the lighthouse to the top of the beach. Pick your spot and drive there.

TACKLE SHOP

● *The Ramsey Warehouse, 37 Parliament St, Ramsey, tel Tel: 01624 813092.*

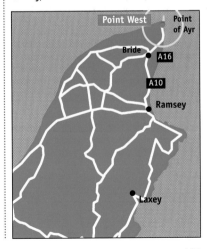

■ *East Tarbet (top) offers several rough ground rock marks for dogfish, conger eel and wrasse.*

The best mark on the south side is Flat Rock, halfway to Mull of Galloway, and consists of rough ground close in, running onto mud and sand with patches of kelp.

West Tarbet is a steep drop into the bay and most of the fishing is from rocks to the south side, which gives deeper water. It is a tackle graveyard.

SPECIES
Dogfish, conger, bull huss, wrasse, flatfish, pollack, coalfish, mackerel and rockling.

BEST BAITS
Most fish baits, worms, and hardback crabs.

TACKLE
Standard medium ground gear is needed. Use single hook traces on the rough ground. Spinning can take pollack and mackerel.

GETTING THERE
Take the A77 from Stranraer to Portpatrick, then the A716 to Drummore. Follow the signs to Mull of Galloway, cross the cattle grid and East Tarbet is on the left and West Tarbet on the right. You can park on the verge between the cattle grid and the lighthouse and walk to your right to the marks.

TACKLE SHOP
● *The Sports Shop, 86 George St, Stranraer, Tel: 01776 702705.*

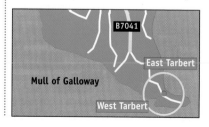

■ *The esplanade at Greenock is a popular venue because you can park and fish next to your car. It can get busy at weekends.*

Evening fishing on a flood tide produces the best results. The venue is noted for good bags of coalfish and flounder, with the latter caught within 50 yards. Distance casting is important for the coalies. The south end is better for dab and codling because the water is deeper with a shelf about 80 yards out. Most fish are caught just beyond this shelf.

SPECIES
Coalfish, flounder, codling and dab.

BEST BAITS
For bait, use peeler crabs for the coalies, lugworms or ragworms for flounder, peelers or white rag for dab.

TACKLE
Standard beach tackle can be used at Greenock esplanade, or if you prefer, even a specialist flounder rod will work. Two or three-hook paternoster rigs, clipped or unclipped, are best. Aberdeen pattern hooks are favoured.

GETTING THERE
From Glasgow, follow the M8 and join the A8, which takes you into Greenock. If approaching from the Largs direction, you should follow the A78 into Greenock.

TACKLE SHOPS
● *The Fishing Shop, 24 Union St, Greenock, Tel: 01475 888085.*

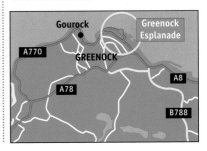

■ *Largs is a typical west coast sea-front town and is busy in summer with visiting tourists. Anglers can expect summer and winter action with a variety of species. The town of Largs is sheltered by the island of Great Cumbrae, making it a safe anchorage and popular sailing centre.*

The deep left-hand side of the point gives way to a mixed bottom of sand, rock and weed below 70ft-80ft of water. Here dogfish are the main species. Casting from the right side finds a sandbank and water that is much shallower, about 15ft-20ft deep. A predominantly low-water mark, the shingle point produces two hours down and three hours up.

SPECIES

Flounder, coalfish, dogfish and codling are species caught at Largs shingle point. July to September is the peak season at this mark, and is best for large numbers of dogfish. The winter season, from November onwards, is best for codling. Mackerel can be feathered from the point throughout the summer.

BEST BAITS

Ragworms, sandeels and mackerel strip are the top dogfish baits. Lug, rag and peeler crabs can be used to catch flounder, coalfish and codling.

TACKLE

Medium beach rods 6500-sized reels are more than adequate here. Use 15lb-18lb mainline with appropriate shockleaders and 150g lead weights.

At this mark, distance casting is not a priority and two or three-hook flapping rigs with size 1 Aberdeen hooks are the norm. Scale down to a size 2 for flounder.

GETTING THERE

From the north and south, take the A75 along the west coast to Largs. The shingle point is obvious from the town promenade and its low-water extremity is pinpointed by a single concrete stanchion.

TACKLE SHOP

● *Hastie of Largs, 109 Main St, Largs, Tel: 01475 673104.*

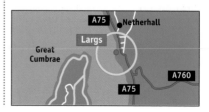

■ *The Mull of Galloway is a venue where tope are hooked and shark are seen regularly.*

There is always a tide running past the point and at times it is strong enough to be like a river in spate and the sea bed can be snaggy. The rocks below, by the lighthouse foghorn, can be productive for pollack, wrasse, dogfish and conger. Be warned however – this is a stiff climb.

SPECIES
Dogfish, conger, bull huss, wrasse, flatfish, pollack, coalfish, mackerel and rockling.

BEST BAITS
Most fish baits, worms and hardback crabs.

TACKLE
Medium-ground gear is best at this mark. Use single hook traces in the rough ground. Spinning can be productive for pollack. Mackerel can be taken on feathers or spinners from early May through to September.

GETTING THERE
Take the A77 from Stranraer to Portpatrick, then the A716 to Drummore. Follow the signs to Mull of Galloway. Go up to the lighthouse car park and leave your vehicle, then follow the path to the point and make your way down the rock face.

TACKLE SHOP
● *The Sports Shop, 86 George St, Stranraer, Tel: 01776 702705.*

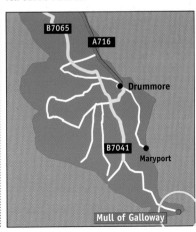

■ *Port Logan is considered a small-boat fishing area, but you can fish across the bay from the harbour. The bottom has a few sandy patches with heavy kelp in places.*

The beach here is sandy, with long gullies running out to rough kelp beds, and is best fished down to low water and two hours up. Casts of 80 yards will reach the fish. You can wade out to cast because the water is shallow at low tide. Sport improves at night.

There are numerous fishing spots among the steep rocks of the Mull of Logan, which offer deep water and a rough bottom. The Bowl is the best hollow with high rocks at both ends. The ebb tide pulls south to north and the flood is the reverse.

SPECIES
Dogfish, coalfish, pollack, codling, wrasse, rockling, conger, flatfish, occasional huss and a chance of bass.

BEST BAITS
Lugworms, ragworms, crabs or fish baits.

TACKLE
Locals use 15lb running line with a shockleader with two-hook traces and a grip lead. Float fishing from the rocks with rag or a sandeel will take pollack and coalfish, but better pollack fall to an artificial eel. Casts of 80 yards reach clearer ground. Otherwise use a single hook rig with grip lead.

GETTING THERE
From the south, take the A75 from Carlisle to Stranraer. Two miles from Glenluce bypass, turn left on the A715 to Sandhead and join the A716 to Drummore. Turn right three miles beyond Ardwell village onto the B7065 to Port Logan. Parking is at a picnic area opposite the beach or at the harbour.

For the Mull of Logan: At the old school, just before the beach at Port Logan, take the right onto Farm Road. It's about two miles to the farmyard. Park in the yard, but ask permission to cross the land, which is normally given. Go through the gate to the right and across the three fields to the steep rocks.

TACKLE SHOP
● *The Sports Shop, 86 George St, Stranraer, Tel: 01776 702705.*

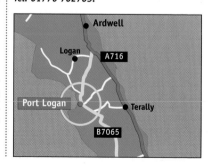

■ *Terally Bay is a steep shingle mark that runs onto sand and bands of weed. It fishes best over high water with a sea running.*

Most species are caught here, with the addition of bass and pollack to the northern end of the bay next to the rocky outcrop. Mackerel come within 10 yards in summer.

SPECIES
Dogfish, plaice, dab, flounder, tub gurnard, mackerel, bass and pollack. Small codling and whiting in winter.

BEST BAITS
Ragworms, lugworms, fish or crabs.

TACKLE
Two-hook traces with a wired lead is the norm here. Spinning with lures and feathers takes bass at times.

GETTING THERE
Take the A75 from Carlisle to Stranraer/Glenluce bypass and the A715 to Sandhead on the A716. Go through Ardwell village and on towards Drummore, past the New England Bay caravan site. Terally Bay is the next bay on the left. Park in the lay-by or at the southern end of the bay.

TACKLE SHOP
● *The Sports Shop, 86 George St, Stranraer, Tel: 01776 702705.*

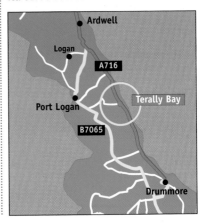

■ *Achiltibuie pier is one of the few marks with a proven track record of producing fish weighing more than 100lb.*

This rock-strewn mark overlooking the Summer Isles has the potential to produce the goods, as proved by a common skate of 154lb caught here in 1971.

Skate fishing has made a comeback on the west coast of Scotland, mainly from the boat. Best time for fishing is June to October, but fish are caught all year.

SPECIES
Besides skate, expect pollack, mackerel and wrasse from the high round surrounding the pier, while the adjacent shingle beach produces dogfish and flatfish.

BEST BAITS
Big fish baits for the common skate, with ragworms for other species.

TACKLE
Float fishing for pollack and wrasse can be done with a light outfit, used for drifting ragworms close to the rocks. Skate fishing would involve a heavy outfit capable of a good cast.

GETTING THERE
Take the A835 north from Ullapool for nine miles until signposts for Achiltibuie appear on the left. Follow the single track road for 15 miles and you can find the pier on the right as you enter the village.

TACKLE SHOP
● *Rod & Gun Shop, High St, Fort William, Tel: 01397 702656.*

AIRD POINT
Eye Peninsula, Lewis, Northwest Scotland

■ *Aird Point on the Isle of Lewis offers clean ground sport to the north and rough to the south. Fish are caught in deep water over all states of the tide, but the flood is the best.*

June through to December produces the best catches. Take care during easterly swells.

Aird Point is on the Eye Peninsula, which is almost an island within an island. Various small roads lead to many surprises in a picturesque area. Nearby St Columba's Church is the old burial ground of the Macleod chiefs of Lewis and the Mackenzies of Seaforth.

SPECIES
Coalfish, dab, dogfish and a few plaice are caught to the north, while coalies, pollack, conger, dogfish, ling, codling, mackerel and wrasse are found to the south.

BEST BAITS
Mackerel, peeler crabs, lugworms and squid work well, but pirks and lures can be successful.

TACKLE
Deep water and strong tides mean 5oz and 6oz grip leads are required, with 20lb mainline.

GETTING THERE
Take the A866 east from Stornoway towards Tiumpan Head on the Eye Peninsula. Turn right at the sign for Aird and park at the road end. The mark is a five-minute walk away.

Holiday visitors to the Isle of Lewis should take the ferry from Ullapool or fly to Stornoway.

TACKLE SHOP
● **Rod & Gun Shop, High St, Fort William, Tel: 01397 702656.**

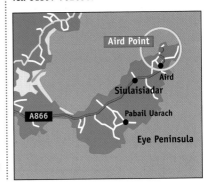

■ *This is the mark made famous by catches of record-breaking common skate from the shore. A British shore record fish of 138lb was caught here in 1989, then a 168lb 8oz skate and the current record of 169lb 6oz was set in 1994.*

Loch Roag is on the western side of the Isle of Lewis and is a large harbour area, which offers easy access to the waters of the Atlantic Ocean. The loch is divided into East and West Roag by the Island of Bernera.

Breascleit pier, on East Loch Roag, has depths varying from 2.5 metres at the inner end to 5.4m at the outer end. The town of Stornoway, capital of the Outer Hebrides, with its harbour, ferry and airport is 17 miles from Breasclete.

Autumn is the best time for common skate to 100lb on rising evening tides, plus thornback ray and dogfish. High water coinciding with darkness is considered the best time to fish.

SPECIES
Thornback ray and dogfish are caught from late June until November. August and September are the best times to try catching a common skate.

BEST BAITS
Mackerel and herring are the best baits.

TACKLE
Casts of 30 yards to 100 yards will put your bait in 40 feet of water on a muddy sea bed. Heavy tackle is required, especially for the big skate.

GETTING THERE
From Stornoway you should follow the A859 before taking a right turn on to the A858 to Callanish and then Breasclete.

TACKLE SHOP
● *Rod & Gun Shop, High St, Fort William, Tel: 01397 702656.*

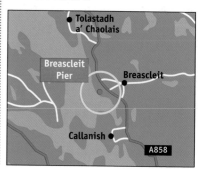

170

■ *The sea bed off Fort William car park is clear with a few snags and anglers can enjoy some easy sport from the car door if required.*

Fort William is the largest town in the west Highlands of Scotland and is the commercial centre of Lochaber, an area renowned for magnificent scenery with an important history. The highest mountain in the UK, Ben Nevis, and Loch Morar, the deepest loch, are nearby.

Construction started in 2001 on an artificial reef in Loch Linnhe, made from 1.25 million concrete blocks weighing 42,000 tonnes. The reef is manufactured from quarry by-products, and when completed, it will be the largest artificial reef in the world.

SPECIES
July to October is the best time for fish when a cast of 60 to 70 yards catches mackerel, thornback ray, dogfish, dab, flounder, whiting, small codling and loads of sea trout.

BEST BAITS
Peeler crabs are the best bait for thornback ray, which range between 2lb and 9lb. Sandeels are good for catching mackerel and dogfish, while worms are used for other species.

TACKLE
A robust rod and 7000-size reel loaded with 20lb mainline is commonly used because ray can be caught two at a time. Use a one-up, one-down rig with 30lb snood lengths and size 1/0 and 2/0 hooks.

The moderate tide in the area pushes hardest at the start of the ebb and 150g to 170g leads are adequate to hold bottom.

GETTING THERE
Fort William is situated on the west-facing bank of Loch Linnhe. From the south, follow the A82 to the town and turn left at the roundabout into the car park.

TACKLE SHOP
● *Rod & Gun Shop, High St, Fort William, Tel: 01397 702656.*

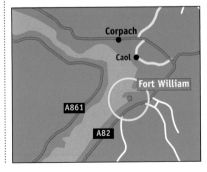

■ *The rocky edges of this deep water sea loch offer numerous accessible outcrops where depths vary from 60ft-120ft at the edge, while casting out around 100 yards locates depths varying from 100-300ft in places.*

Late April to October is best for codling. Two hours either side of bottom water after spring tides is most productive for codling. Wrasse fishing is best between July and October. Dogfish are present all year.

SPECIES
Codling, dogfish, wrasse, pouting, whiting, pollack, poor cod, coalfish and strap conger. Pollack and sea trout closer to the castle.

BEST BAITS
Peeler crabs, lugworms, ragworms and mussels will catch codling and wrasse. Mackerel head or whole calamari squid for conger. Sandeels and mackerel for dogfish. Rag, sandeels and

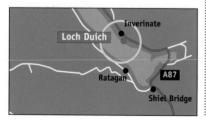

artificials tempt pollack. Loose feeding anything from mashed crabs to limpets prompts the wrasse to feed.

TACKLE
It is best to carry a set up for general fishing and another lighter one for pollack. Any beachcaster with a 6oz rating will do, but a fairly large capacity reel is essential. Use 20lb mainline with a casting leader on a strong multiplier or 30lb braided line on a large fixed-spool reel.

A two-hook trace with size 2/0 hooks on 25lb snoods is a good all-rounder. Congers require a single 80lb snood and a size 6/0 hook. Grip leads are optional. Pay attention to the angle of your line which creeps back towards you as the weight settles.

Sliding float rigs, artificial eel, spinners, plugs and live baits on 4ft-6ft traces all work when fishing for pollack.

GETTING THERE
Follow the A87 past Shiel Bridge to the north Loch Duich shoreline. Gaps in the barriers allow cars to be parked off the road at locations all along the north side. There is also parking at Eilean Donan Castle.

TACKLE SHOP
● *Rod & Gun Shop, High St, Fort William, Tel: 01397 702656.*

■ *Once famous for big catches of cod, this part of the Gare Loch is now a top mark for dogfish, with other species being codling, dab and whiting.*

The point to the rear of the white house, the stony beach to the right, and the first 200 yards up to the rocks on the left are most popular.

Dogfish begin to appear in reasonable numbers from April. Night fishing brings better catches into summer, with the top sport over low water.

SPECIES
Dogfish, codling, dab and whiting.

BEST BAITS
Combinations of ragworms, sandeels and fresh fish are the main dogfish baits, but a few peeler crabs are useful for codling.

TACKLE
Two or three-hook unclipped rigs with 18in snoods are ideal. Use 150g or 170g breakout leads to handle the strongest tides. Mainline should be 60lb and a long shockleader.

A cast of 40 yards will put dogfish baits over an underwater ledge at low water, with 75 yards required at top water. After casting out, don't return your rod to the rest. Hold it and pay our plenty of line allowing time for your lead to hit bottom. Tidal pull is strong around mid-tide, when tackle losses can become severe.

GETTING THERE
Take the A814 through Helensburgh to Garelochhead, then go left on the B833 to Mambeg. The mark is about a mile from the Kilcreggan turnoff.

This roadside mark is signposted and a white house is the only landmark for the rock point and adjoining stretches. There is no room to park, with perhaps only six cars able to stop by the road 50 yards from the house. Do not park in the private spaces allocated for residents.

TACKLE SHOP
● *Glasgow Angling Centre, 6 Claythorn St, Gallowgate, Glasgow, Tel: 0141 552 1447.*

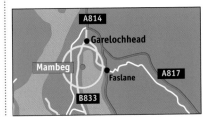

■ *A well-known mark capable of producing bags of big cod, this beach can seem almost fishless unless the conditions are spot on.*

Fishing between October and March, a high tide in darkness with the sea falling after an easterly wind is best for double-figure cod. The middle to north end of this small pebble beach is usually the most productive area.

SPECIES
Cod, coalfish , flounder and the odd strap eel.

BEST BAITS
Lugworms tipped with razorfish, mussels or crabs are all popular baits for Auchmithie beach. The locally-favoured 'whole squid and wait' approach sorts out the bigger fish.

TACKLE
Heavy gear is needed because the rough ground and weather will find any weakness in standard tackle. A Pennell rig carrying size 3/0 or 4/0 Viking hooks, rotten bottom and grip weight will be best fished off 40 lb mainline. Most of the fish are located at close range.

GETTING THERE.
Signposted on the main A92 from the outskirts of Arbroath, Auchmithie sits on top of the cliffs. The road down to the beach carries warnings because it can be dangerous. Parking at the top and following the path down on foot can be the best option.

TACKLE SHOP
● *Arbroath Cycle and Tackle, 274 High St, Arbroath, Tel: 01241 873467.*

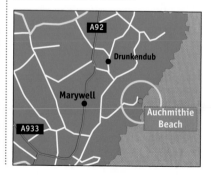

■ *Easy access and good rough ground sport help make this a popular mark with travelling anglers. Cod and bass dominate, but plenty of wrasse and coalfish keep the rod tips nodding.*

Best sport is from late September through to early April, with the best cod caught in January. Low water and the first two hours of the flood are most productive.

Boddin offers shelter from the worst of the winter weather whichever way the sea is running. Fish from low water up on the north side, then switch to the southern side over high.

SPECIES

Double-figure cod are the main target all year, but coalfish boost sport. The north side is better for cod in summer and the south is usually opted for early morning by bass anglers.

BEST BAITS

Best results for cod use a large lug-based cocktail or frozen crabs.

TACKLE

Cod run to 10lb, so use a size 3/0 or 4/0 pulley rig or Pennell rig and rotten-bottom link. Cast into the thick kelp 30-40 yards from the shore.

Use a larger edible or velvet soft crabs on a similar rig for bass.

GETTING THERE

Follow signs for Usan from the main A92 and Boddin is signposted after around 500 yards. Park at the side of the track overlooking the sea.

TACKLE SHOP

● *Cobsport, 7 Castle Street, Montrose,*
Tel: 01674 673095.

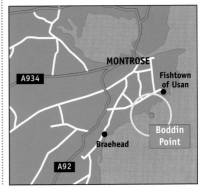

175

■ *The rougher the better in winter at this mark because the open sea becomes unfishable and the shelter here makes it a favourite venue for cod. Best marks are at the seaward end, but cod are caught right up to the bridges at Montrose. Although big cod are the main target, plenty of codling and coalfish also show.*

The season runs from mid-October to early March and peaks in the bad storms. The first three weeks of the year is best for bigger cod.

Summer fishing is mostly over slack water at either side of the tide owing to the difficulties caused by the fast-flowing water emptying from the basin. The bottom is mixed, with very muddy areas bordering weed beds and some snaggy, rocky ground.

SPECIES
Cod, coalfish, flounder and eel.

BEST BAITS
Peeler crabs, ragworms and mussels.

TACKLE
Use three hooks flapping for flounder and eel with ragworms and peeler crabs the top baits. Use a size 3/0 Pennell pulley rig baited with a large shellfish and lug cocktail for winter cod. Rotten-bottoms are an optional extra. Fish are mostly found in the rougher ground at your feet with casting a distinct disadvantage.

The top method for summer codling and coalfish is a single size 2/0 Aberdeen hook baited with mussels or crabs. A rotten-bottom can be useful, but is not always needed.

Casting more than 30 or 40 yards makes it almost impossible to hold bottom at this mark, although more fish are located on the edge of the tide race.

GETTING THERE
The main A92 runs through Montrose and Ferryden is signposted from the roundabout at the southern end of town. Follow this road keeping the water on your left and the road ends in a small car park.

TACKLE SHOP
● *Cobsport, 7 Castle Place, Montrose, Tel: 01674 673095.*

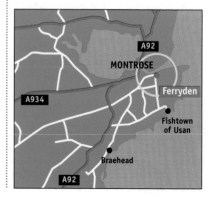

■ *At Inverbervie, cod to double figures can be taken along the length of the pebble beach during easterly seas in winter.*

The season runs from October to February peaking in January. Weed can be a big problem during the first storms of the winter and fishing can be impossible.

Night tides over high will see fish at all ranges with the gutter about 40 yd out particularly productive. Midweek sessions where practical are often better as this beach becomes very crowded during ideal conditions.

SPECIES
Cod, flounder and coalfish

BEST BAITS
Razorfish and crab cocktail is a favourite, but most recognised cod baits work.

TACKLE
Standard gear will be sufficient during calmer spells at this mark, but heavier gear will be needed from the rocks during rougher weather. A long rubbing leader can help, as can a rotten bottom because the rocks and pebbles can move about quite a lot during ideal conditions.

Use a Pennell rig with size 3/0 hooks to present the large baits, while grip lead weights are essential most of the time.

GETTING THERE
The main A92 coast road runs through Inverbervie and the beach is signposted both ways from it. There is ample parking on top of the beach, at the car park.

TACKLE
● *Cobsport, 7 Castle Street, Montrose, Tel: 01674 673095.*

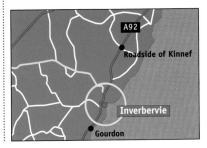

■ *The area from Tayport to Balmerino is made up of rocky outcrops and deep mud shallow water bays. Fishing is mainly confined to the summer only, with May to September generally regarded as the months for best results.*

Low water tends to concentrate the fish in the gullies and fishing at close range is best. Groundbaiting can help, but this is best done with the help of the ebb tide.

SPECIES
Flounder, eel, small codling and coalfish with a chance of a bass at dusk or dawn.

BEST BAITS
Ragworms and fish baits will catch plenty of early-season fish, but remember that once the crab moult gets into full swing, only top quality peeler crabs will do.

TACKLE
Bass or flattie rods and 12lb line are ideal until the tide begins to push hard, then a standard beachcaster and grip weight anchored on the

edge of the tide is best. Three size 2, fine-wire hooks fished flapping at close range is the norm.

GETTING THERE
The A92 Tay Road bridge almost splits the area in two and turning toward Wormit and Tayport from the bridge gives you the plenty of choice of where to fish. The marks underneath the bridge are a good starting point for first-time visitors.

TACKLE SHOP
● *Anglers Choice, High St, Lochee,*
Tel: 01382 400555.

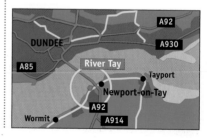

■ *Typical of many rock marks in the area, The Crawton fishes best throughout the winter for cod, with summertime offering more variety with a number of rough ground species likely.*

Winter runs from October to March with a seasonal lull till the weather settles around June when fishing in the kelp really takes off.

SPECIES

Cod, coalfish, wrasse, strap eel and pollack. Occasional mackerel shoals can show during autumn evenings.

BEST BAITS

Lugworms tipped with a piece of crab will be the standard winter cod bait, with mussels, razorfish and squid good for tipping off. Fish crabs only for cod in summer. Fish strip and ragworms will be useful summer additions for other species.

TACKLE

Bottom fishing throughout the year will see heavy gear and big Pennell rigs a must. The addition of a float rod is a sporting alternative for wrasse and pollack in summer.

GETTING THERE

There is one signposted turning from the main A92 coast road that takes you to a car park at the top of The Crawton's main gully.

TACKLE SHOP

● *Cobsport, Castle Terrace, Montrose, Tel: 01674 673095.*

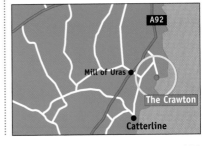

DUNBAR EAST BEACH
East Lothian, Southeast Scotland

■ *This gently-sloping beach is a mixture of pebbles and coarse sand that eventually recedes on to mostly rock and kelp.*

A strip of clear sand, which extends well out, is located by following the main timber groyne towards the low water mark. Casting to where kelp meets the sand is often the key to good results. There is 12 feet of water behind the kelp at the bottom of a spring tide.

SPECIES
Night fishing from October to February produces cod following onshore storms. May to September yields kelp codling and fresh cod.

An hour down and two up over low water on springs is best for summer codling and wrasse. Flounders are caught from July to November, with the biggest fish taken from the sand after a period of onshore weather. Small coalfish are the other main species.

BEST BAITS
Peeler crabs out-fish all other cod baits in summer, while cocktails of lugworms, ragworms, white rag, razorfish, mussels and squid take over between November and February.

Peelers are also a key bait for flounders, but rag, lug and mackerel strip can be used. If you are short of bait, some good lugworms can be dug from the sand.

TACKLE
When fishing at this mark, tick to strong tackle, such as a beach rod capable of casting 6oz, matched with a sturdy reel.

Mainlines should be robust, either a standard 30lb mono straight through or a low diameter with appropriate shockleader. A single-hook trace with a 3ft trailing snood is best. Rotten-bottom links are not essential, but most anglers use them. Size 1/0-4/0 Kamasan B940 hooks cover most eventualities.

Anglers targeting flounder can opt for a lighter outfit with two or three-hook rigs carrying size 1 or 2 Limericks.

GETTING THERE
Leave the A1 at the Beltonford roundabout and drive into Dunbar. The East Beach runs parallel to the main street. Cars can be parked in the arcade car park.

TACKLE SHOP
● *Cromwell Marine Ltd, Cromwell Harbour, Shore St, Dunbar, Tel: 01368 863354.*

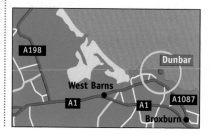

■ *The area is a rough ground angler's paradise with plenty of cod among the snags. Rock fingers and craggy skeers take on a dense blanket of kelp cover close to the low water extremity.*

Cod are the main species in both summer and winter. Fish can be taken at any stage of the tide, but two hours down to low water and the bottom three hours of the flood give best results.

Winter cod sport builds up from November and peaks during January and February, when double-figure fish are common among the smaller fish taken at night.

Summer codling run from 1lb-6lb and display a deep red coloration. A good daylight haul from mid-June to September may well exceed 50lb.

Moving as little as 10 yards along the mark can make a huge difference in catches. This is because there are numerous gullies and holes where fish like to congregate at certain states of the tide.

SPECIES
Mainly cod, but you can also expect coalfish and ballan wrasse.

BEST BAITS
Peeler crabs are most effective bait during summer, also accounting for coalfish and ballan wrasse. Lugworms, mussels and frozen peelers are the top winter baits.

TACKLE
Stout tackle and a firm hand are needed to ensure hooked fish are steered safely ashore. A low diameter 30lb-35lb mainline is essential and rigs should be compact and disposable.

A Pennell rig made with size 2/0 to 5/0 Viking hooks, with a rotten-bottom and a 5oz or 6oz lead weight are sufficient. Long casting is unnecessary because more fish are caught close in than further out.

You also need a pair of chest waders and a rucksack holdall.

GETTING THERE
Fife Ness nestles between Crail and St Andrews. Follow the A917 from Anstruther, turning right into the old airstrip at the signs advertising the mini cart track. Follow the road down to the lip of the fishing mark and park alongside or close to the old concrete pillbox.

TACKLE SHOP
● *Joe's Tackle, Buckhaven,*
Tel: 01592 713532.

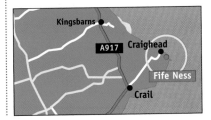

181

HAWES PIER, SOUTH QUEENSBURY
Edinburgh, Southeast Scotland

■ *This pier is overlooked by the road and rail bridges spanning the River Forth between South and North Queensferry.*

The left-hand side of the pier is generally regarded as the most productive. There are plenty of flounder, eel and small blennies.

The whole of the flood and first few hours of the ebb are best. June to October is the most consistent time for flounder and eel. Warm summer evenings can sometimes produce a few mackerel when using feathers.

Onshore easterly or north-easterly winds can give odd codling at night during the winter, but long casting is required.

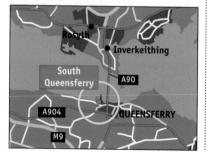

SPECIES
Flounder, eel and codling.

BEST BAITS
Use small ragworms, harbour rag and white rag or a peeler crab tipped with these. Twitching baits back a few inches every five minutes can entice fish to feed.

TACKLE
Light tackle, such as a carp or bass rod, and fixed-spool reel makes this mark fun to fish. Use 10lb-15lb mainline and a 3oz rolling bomb to hold bottom.

A two-hook paternoster with 24in hook snoods is highly rated. Use size 2 or size 4 fine-wire hooks for best results.

GETTING THERE
From the main A90, turn off for Dalmeny and South Queensferry, following the road to South Queensferry shore. The Hawes pier sits opposite the Hawes Inn.

TACKLE SHOP
● *Mike's Tackle Shop, 46 Portobello High St, Edinburgh, Tel: 0131 657 3258.*

■ Winter codling are the mainstay from North Berwick's rocky marks. An extensive reef system exists behind the town's small harbour and it is here that that anglers target double-figure cod. The area from the harbour mouth to the rear of the old open-air swimming pool produces codling after strong north-easterly winds. Don't ignore this area between May and September because good bags of codling can be caught on peeler crabs. The harbour marks are safe in all but the strongest onshore gales.

Night fishing between October to February is the best time to seek cod to 15lb. Wrasse, coalfish, odd pollack and flounder can be expected as well throughout summer and autumn.

SPECIES
Cod, coalfish, wrasse, flounder as well as the occasional pollack.

BEST BAITS
Peeler crabs are best until October. Generous cocktails of lugworms, king rag, snake white rag, mussels, razorfish, frozen peeler crabs and squid work well either side of Christmas.

TACKLE
Strong tackle and a heavy mainline is necessary to drag fish from the extremely rough ground.

A rotten bottom attachment or pulley rig with a 30in hooklength of 35lb mono is best. Size 2/0-3/0 hooks cover early fishing for codling, but it's a good idea to step up to a single 4/0 hook or Pennell in winter.

If you don't lose a few leads then you are fishing in the wrong place. Breakout leads will help keep loses to an acceptable level because they stick and won't roll into crevices.

GETTING THERE
From the A1, take the A198 into the centre of North Berwick. The harbour is clearly signposted and cars can be parked at the quayside.

TACKLE SHOP
● *Mike's Tackle Shop, 46 Portobello High St, Edinburgh, Tel: 0131 657 3258.*

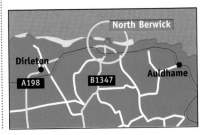

■ *St Andrews rocks are popular with winter cod anglers, but can produce excellent summer results for flounder, plaice and bass.*

Cod in winter can reach double figures and they prefer the colour and sea movement associated with onshore winds. Summer sport runs between June and September, with the winter season running from October to March, but this is very dependent on the weather.

Summer sport is best left to the early mornings or evenings when the tourists are less likely to be about. Cod in the summer are far more predictable in the kelp gullies, but if variety is preferred then stick to the edges of the rough ground where the beach meets the rocks.

SPECIES
Mainly cod, flounder, plaice and bass.

BEST BAITS
Winter fish prefer a cocktail bait. Lugworms, razorfish, mussels and crabs are the essentials. Crabs are the top summer bait, with ragworms a handy standby for flatfish.

TACKLE
Winter means heavy gear, rotten bottoms and fast-retrieve reels, although casting can be useful as the sea settles after onshore conditions. Use 20lb line and a shockleader. Summer cod in the kelp also demand heavy gear, but standard gear will handle the mixed ground.

GETTING THERE
The A91 runs through St Andrews and the rocks run the length of the town. Access to these is perhaps easiest near the sealife centre.

TACKLE SHOP
● *Anglers Creel, 33 Exchange Street, Dundee, Tel: 01382 205075.*

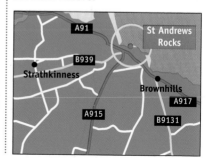

■ *These weedy rock and boulder fingers lie between Port Edgar marina and the grounds of Hopetoun House.*

Take a look at the beach on a big spring tide to see where the mud gives way to firm sand.

A cast of around 40 yards is normally adequate. If the fishing is slow, it is better to move rather than try and blast your baits out.

This area fishes best on a big tide, when catches of a dozen or more decent flounder and a few eels is not uncommon. The whole of the flood produces fish, but the first two or three hours are usually best. Bass tend to be caught close in over high water.

Fish are caught most months, but the period between June and October is best.

SPECIES
Flounder, eel and bass.

BEST BAITS
Peeler crabs are good for flounder and eel, but ragworms are better for bass. Ragworms tipped with small pieces of fish take flounder when crabs are scarce.

TACKLE
Chest or thigh waders are essential. Use a rod with an optimum casting weight of 150g and small multiplier reel loaded with 15lb line. A bass rod and fixed-spool can be used on the smaller tides. A simple three-hook flapping rig with size 2 hooks covers all options. You will need to use grip leads on the bigger tides.

GETTING THERE
Follow the signs for Hopetoun House from South Queensferry. The Society Points are situated several hundred yards before the entrance to the estate.

TACKLE SHOP
● *Mike's Tackle Shop, 46 Portobello High St, Edinburgh, Tel: 0131 657 3258.*

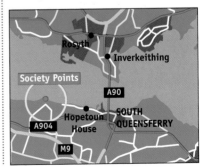

185

Index

The Top Marks are entered here under their individual names, and also separately under their respective county headings.

A

Aberdaron Beach 128
Achiltibuie Pier 168
Admiralty Pier 66
Afon Wen Beach 129
Aird Point 169
Aldeburgh Town Beach 54
Alderney Breakwater 96
Alnmouth Bridge 10
Anderby Creek 42
Atwick 34
Auchmithie Beach 174
Aust 114
Axmouth 100

B

Beadnell 11
Beckfoot 152
Beltinge Promenade 67
Bembridge Harbour 84
Blackhall 22
Blast Beach 26
Boddin Point 175
Bog Hall Rocks 13
Brean Down 115
Breascleit Pier 170
Brighton Marina 72
Brixham Breakwater 101

C

Caister-on-Sea 49
Caldy 140
Cambois Rocks 12
Castle Beach 130
Chale Bay 85
Challaborough 102

Channel Islands 96–99
    Alderney Breakwater 96
    Gorey Harbour 97
        Sorel Point 98
        St Catherine's Breakwater 99
Chemical Beach 25
Clevedon 116

Cleveland 28–33
    Hummersea 28
    Saltburn Pier 29
    The Heugh 30
    Staincliff Hotel 31
    Redcar East Scaurs 32
    North & South Gare 33
Cleveleys 146
Cliff End, Pett Levels 73
Cliff Road 60
Cloughton Wyke 35
Colwyn Bay Promenade 134

Cornwall 108–113
    Cremyll Battery 108
    Polhawn Cove 109
    Porthcurno 110
    The Island 111
    The Merlin 112
    Treyarnon Bay 113

County Durham 22–27
    Blackhall 22
    Easington Beach 23
    Crimdon 24
    Chemical Beach 25
    Blast Beach 26
    Horden 27
Craster Harbour 15
Cremyll Battery 108
Crimdon 24
Cullercoats 17

Cumbria 152–157
    Beckfoot 152
    Dubmill Point 153
    Maryport Harbour 154
    Nethertown 155
    Silloth 156
    Whitehaven Piers 157

D
Devon 100–107
  Axmouth 100
  Brixham Breakwater 101
  Challaborough 102
  Lion's Den 103
  Mothecombe 104
  Princess & Haldon Piers 105
  Seaton 106
  Teign Estuary 107
Dinas Dinlle 131
Dunbar East Beach 180

Dorset 88–95
  Durdle Door 88
  Friars Cliff Beach 89
  Jerry's Point 91
  Ringstead Bay 92
  Southbourne 93
  Swanage Pier 94
  West Bexington 95
Dover Southern Breakwater 68
Dovercourt Beach 61
Dubmill Point 153
Durdle Door 88

E
Easington Beach 23
East And West Tarbet 162

Essex 60–65
  Cliff Road 60
  Dovercourt Beach 61
  Frinton Wall 62
  Halfpenny Pier 63
  River Crouch 64
  Southend-on-Sea Pier 65

F
Ferryden 176
Fife Ness 181
Filey Brigg 40
Folkestone Pier 69
Fort William 171
Friars Cliff Beach 89

Frinton Wall 62

G
Gansey 158
Gorey Harbour 97
Great Yarmouth North Beach 51
Greenock Esplanade 163

H
Halfpenny Pier 63
Hamble Common 78

Hampshire 78–83
  Hamble Common 78
  Hurst Shingle Bank 79
  Lee-on-the-Solent 80
  Lepe Beach 81
  Long Groyne 90
  Southsea 82
  Weston Shore 83
Hastings Harbour Arm 74
Hawes Pier, South Queensbury 182
Hayburn Wyke 39
Hinkley Point 117
Holyhead Breakwater 135
Horden 27
Hummersea 28
Hurst Shingle Bank 79

I
Ingoldmells Point 43
Inverbervie 177

Isle of Man 158–161
  Gansey 158
  Langness 159
  Manx Match 160
  Point West 161

Isle of Wight 84–87
  Bembridge Harbour 84
  Chale Bay 85
  River Medina 86
  Yarmouth Pier 87

J
Jarrow 18
Jerry's Point 91

K
Kent 66–71
  Admiralty Pier 66
  Beltinge Promenade 67
  Dover Southern Breakwater 68
  Folkestone Pier 69
  Marine Parade 70
  Reculver Towers 71
Knab Rock 120

L
Lancashire 146–11
  Cleveleys 146
  Lytham 147
  Marine Beach 148
  Morecambe 149
  Rossall Point 150
  Stanah 151
Landguard Beach 55
Langness 159
Largs Shingle Point 164
Lee-on-the-Solent 80
Lepe Beach 81

Lincolnshire 42–47
  Anderby Creek 42
  Ingoldmells Point 43
  Saltfleet Haven 44
  Sutton On Sea 45
  Wolla Bank 46
  Mablethorpe 47
Lion's Den 103
Llandudno Pier 136
Llanmadoc 121
Loch Duich North Shore 172
Long Groyne 90
Lowestoft South Pier 56
Lytham 147

M
Mablethorpe 47
Makro 36
Mambeg 173

Manx Match 160
Marine Beach 148
Marine Parade 70
Maryport Harbour 154

Merseyside 140–145
  Caldy 140
  Otterspool 141
  Perch Rock Beach 142
  Red Rocks 143
  Seaforth Rocks 144
  Vale Park 145
Monknash 123
Monkstone Point 124
Morecambe 149
Mostyn 137
Mothecombe 104
Mull of Galloway 165
Mundesley 52

N
Nethertown 155

Norfolk 48–53
  North & South Eccles 48
  Caister-on-Sea 49
  River Great Ouse 50
  Great Yarmouth North Beach 51
  Mundesley 52
  Sea Palling Reefs 53
North & South Eccles 48
North & South Gare 33
North Berwick 183

North Wales 134–139
  Colwyn Bay Promenade 134
  Llandudno Pier 136
  Mostyn 137
  Rhos-on-Sea 138
  Talacre 139

Northeast Scotland 174–179
  Auchmithie Beach 174
  Boddin Point 175
  Ferryden 176
  Inverbervie 177
  River Tay South Shore 178

The Crawton 179

Northumberland   10–15
    Alnmouth Bridge 10
    Beadnell 11
    Cambois Rocks 12
    Bog Hall Rocks 13
    Seahouses 14
    Craster Harbour 15

Northwest Scotland 168–173
    Achiltibuie Pier 168
    Aird Point 169
    Breascleit Pier 170
    Fort William 171
    Loch Duich North Shore 172
    Mambeg 173

O
Orford Ness 57
Otterspool 141

P
Perch Rock Beach 142
Piddinghoe 75
Point West 161
Polhawn Cove 109
Port Logan 166
Porth Oer 132
Porthcurno 110
Portishead 118
Princess & Haldon Piers 105
Pwllheli South Beach 133

R
Reculver Towers 71
Red Rocks 143
Redcar East Scaurs 32
Rhos-on-Sea 138
Rhossili Beach 125
Ringstead Bay 92
River Crouch 64
River Great Ouse 50
River Medina 86
River Tay South Shore 178
Rossall Point 150
Rottingdean 76

S
Saltburn Pier 29
Saltfleet Haven 44
Saltwick Bay 37
Sand Point 119
Sea Palling Reefs 53
Seaforth Rocks 144
Seahouses 14
Seaton 106
Silloth 156
Sizewell 58
Society Points 185

Somerset & Gloucester 114–119
    Aust 114
    Brean Down 115
    Clevedon 116
    Hinkley Point 117
    Portishead 118
    Sand Point 119
Sorel Point 98
South Hylton 20

South Wales 120–124
    Knab Rock 120
    Llanmadoc 121
    The River Loughor 122
    Monknash 123
    Monkstone Point 124
    Rhossili Beach 125
    St Brides 126
    Sully Island 127
Southbourne 93

Southeast Scotland 180–185
    Dunbar East Beach 180
    Fife Ness 181
    Hawes Pier, South Queensbury 182
    North Berwick 183
    St Andrews Rocks 184
    Society Points 185
Southend-on-Sea Pier 65
Southsea 82

Southwest Scotland 162–167
    East And West Tarbet 162
    Greenock Esplanade 163

Largs Shingle Point 164
Mull Of Galloway 165
Port Logan 166
Terally Bay 167
St Andrews Rocks 184
St Brides 126
St Catherine's Breakwater 99
St Mary's Island 19
Staincliff Hotel 31
Staintondale 38
Stanah 151

Suffolk 54–59
  Aldeburgh Town Beach 54
  Landguard Beach 55
  Lowestoft South Pier 56
  Orford Ness 57
  Sizewell 58
  Thorpeness Point 59
Sully Island 127

Sussex 72–77
  Brighton Marina 72
  Cliff End, Pett Levels 73
  Hastings Harbour Arm 74
  Piddinghoe 75
  Rottingdean 76
  Tidemills 77
Sutton on Sea 45
Swanage Pier 94

T
Talacre 139
Teign Estuary 107
Terally Bay 167
The Black Middens 16
The Crawton 179
The Heugh 30
The Island 111
The Merlin 112
The River Loughor 122
Thorpeness Point 59

Tidemills 77
Treyarnon Bay 113
Tunstall 41

Tyne & Wear 16–21
  The Black Middens 16
  Cullercoats 17
  Jarrow 18
  St Mary's Island 19
  South Hylton 20
  Whitley Bay Beach 21

V
Vale Park 145

W
West Bexington 95

West Wales 128–133
  Aberdaron Beach 128
  Afon Wen Beach 129
  Castle Beach 130
  Dinas Dinlle 131
  Porth Oer 132
  Pwllheli South Beach 133
Weston Shore 83
Whitehaven Piers 157
Whitley Bay Beach 21
Wolla Bank 46

Y
Yarmouth Pier 87

Yorkshire 34–41
  Atwick 34
  Cloughton Wyke 35
  Makro 36
  Saltwick Bay 37
  Staintondale 38
  Hayburn Wyke 39
  Filey Brigg 40
  Tunstall 41

Sea Angler, the magazine that is as important as your fishing tackle!

Britain's biggest selling sea angling monthly is your friendly guiding hand that explains what tackle you should choose, what rigs work best, the top baits to put on the hook and the hottest marks to fish.

With all this regular knowledge you can fish with confidence through the seasons and make the most of all those fishing opportunities.
More information in Sea Angler magazine.

Other Sea Angler 'helping hands'

- Step-by-step guide to Baits and Rigs book
- Sea Angler Bait video – the hands-on guide to presenting the perfect bait
- Sea Angler Rigs video – learn how to tie knots and build rigs the expert way

On sale 18th of every month